S. Stepniak

The Russian Peasantry

Their agrarian Condition, Social Life, and Religion - Vol. I

S. Stepniak

The Russian Peasantry
Their agrarian Condition, Social Life, and Religion - Vol. I

ISBN/EAN: 9783337132422

Printed in Europe, USA, Canada, Australia, Japan

Cover: Foto ©ninafisch / pixelio.de

More available books at **www.hansebooks.com**

THE RUSSIAN PEASANTRY.

VOL. I.

THE RUSSIAN PEASANTRY

*THEIR AGRARIAN CONDITION, SOCIAL
LIFE, AND RELIGION*

BY
STEPNIAK
AUTHOR OF
"THE RUSSIAN STORM-CLOUD," "RUSSIA UNDER THE TSARS"
AND "UNDERGROUND RUSSIA"

VOLUME I.

SECOND  EDITION

LONDON
SWAN SONNENSCHEIN AND CO.
PATERNOSTER SQUARE
1888

Printed by Hazell, Watson, & Viney, Ld., London and Aylesbury.

PREFACE.

THE deep-seated democratic feeling of the whole of our educated classes, which is the mainspring of our political rebellion, has left a well-defined impression upon modern Russian literature. Educated Russians, deprived of any means wherewith to help the people out of their present difficulties, have wanted at least to know all about their condition, and have caught with avidity at any information that men of letters were able to give them.

Hence a unique development of our literature upon this subject. In no other country has so large a number of prominent writers devoted themselves to bringing to light the condition, the needs, and the hopes of the toiling masses; nowhere else have the educated classes given such an unswerving encouragement to similar investigations. The statistical Commissions, instituted by most of our *zemstvos*, have already described the actual position of many millions of peasant households, scattered over an area far surpassing in extent that of the whole of the German Empire, with the same precision and profusion of detail as the reporters of the *Pall Mall Gazette* have devoted to the description of a few blocks of houses in Commercial Street at the time of the Trafalgar Square disturbances. A numerous body of writers, taking various points of view, has carefully elaborated in books and in magazine articles the enormous amount of rough material accumulated in official and non-official publications. Every branch of popular life of any importance, or presenting any complication, has been made a speciality. The village commune has a complete literature of its own. So has popular religion. We have talented writers, like Mrs. A. Efimenko, who have made for themselves a name and a literary position as investigators of the traditional juridical conceptions of our people; or others, like Yousoff, who is an authority upon the modern phase of ritualistic nonconformity.

The works which have most stirred the public mind within the last twenty-five years have been those which have thrown some new light upon popular life: "The Sketches of our National Economy after the Emancipation," by a well-known anonymous author; the "Letters from a Village," by Enghelhardt; a book by Flerovsky, the works of Shapov, and the statistical essays of Professor Yansen. The magazine which for eighteen years of its existence held the foremost place amongst our periodicals, both as regards its circulation and its influence, was one which made the investigation of the life of the people its speciality. Among all the novelists and story-tellers of our generation there is none whose works are read with such avidity as those of Gleb Uspensky on village life.

The extraordinary development and variety of this kind of literature may well be taken as a conclusive proof that, apart from the great taste shown by our public for this class of subject, there must be something really original and worth studying in our rural classes. Neither democratic tendencies nor patriotism could have withstood dulness and insipidity for so long a time.

Our peasants have in fact something unusual about them. They have not lived upon the crumbs of intellectual food which have fallen from the tables of their cultured brethren. Their popular morals, their social aims, and their religion are all their own, and differ greatly from those prevailing with the upper classes.

For the present generation the study of popular life has acquired an exceptional interest and importance, as the manifold influences of the new times have wrought a general downfall of the very basis of rural life. Russian peasants are passing through an actual crisis—economical, social, and religious—and the future of our country depends upon its solution.

In the book we now have the honour to lay before the English reader we have tried to show as briefly and as fully as possible the main features and the bearings of this double process of growth and decay, now to be observed within our rural classes. The task we set ourselves was to choose from among the rich materials scattered throughout our literature for the last score of years, and to arrange the various separate pieces into one general picture. This work is therefore the natural supplement and completion of our two former books, which were devoted to the description of various aspects of the same crisis in the higher, though narrower, walks of our national life.

Most of that which is described in these volumes refers to the bulk of the Russian peasantry; but in dealing with the political views and social habits of our rural classes, and the changes they have undergone since their Emancipation, we have had the Great Russian peasants chiefly in view. It is they who have shaped Russian history in the past, and who will certainly play the leading part in her future.

In conclusion, we beg to acknowledge our obligation to the *Times*, in whose columns the chapters upon the Agrarian Question first appeared; and to the *Fortnightly Review*, which opened its pages to the chapters on "The *Moujiks* and Russian Democracy" (considerably enlarged for the present work), and to the first and third chapters of the section entitled "Paternal Government." The remaining matter, *i.e.*, three-fourths of the entire work, is now published for the first time.

STEPNIAK.

MARCH 1888.

CONTENTS OF VOLUME I.

	PAGE
THE RUSSIAN AGRARIAN QUESTION	1
THE MOUJIKS AND THE RUSSIAN DEMOCRACY	115
PATERNAL GOVERNMENT	151
HARD TIMES	229

THE RUSSIAN AGRARIAN QUESTION.

CHAPTER I.

IN all European countries the agrarian question is of great moment, but in none does it possess the same interest and importance as in Russia. Here the agricultural class constitutes eighty-two per cent. of the entire population, equal for European Russia, exclusive of Finland and Poland, to about sixty-three million souls. Ireland alone, with seventy-three per cent. of her population engaged in husbandry, approaches, at some distance, this figure. Russia is, and must undoubtedly for many years remain, a peasant State in the fullest acceptation of the term. With us, therefore, the agrarian question is the national question, and agrarian concerns are national concerns, all others being dependent on and subservient to them. The tillers of the soil—our *moujiks*—must of necessity become the chief figures in our social and political life. On the *moujik* rests the financial, military, and political power of the State, as well as its interior cohesion and prosperity. The inclinations, ideals, and aspirations of the *moujiks* will also play the principal part in the remoulding of Russia's future. For all interested in politics—statesmen and administrators, writers and scholars—the *moujik* must be the prime object of study, observation, and investigation, as well as of practical manipulation.

For the same reasons the Russian *moujik* has always attracted the attention of observant travellers who have desired to make known to English-speaking readers the agrarian conditions of this strange country, of which so much is said and so little known. There are few among educated foreigners who have not heard of the self-governing, semi-republican *mir* and the somewhat communistic Russian system of land tenure, with its periodical equalizations and divisions. Much less attention has been given by the European public to the modern phases of Russian agrarian life, albeit this side of the question is perhaps the most interesting and instructive.

The Emancipation Act of February 19th, 1861, enfranchising and settling the economical conditions of one-half of our rural population, the former serfs of the nobility, followed in 1866 by a second Act, settling the condition of the other half, the former State peasants, were by far the most extensive experiments in the way of agrarian legislation the world has yet seen. The peculiarities of our traditional system of land tenure, sanctioned to a great extent by the Emancipation Act, imparted to this experiment an additional interest.

That these experiments have not proved a success no competent person can now deny. Emancipation has utterly failed to realize the ardent expectations of its advocates and promoters. The great benefit of the measure was purely moral. It has failed to improve the material condition of the former serfs, who on the whole are worse off than they were before the Emancipation. The bulk of our peasantry is in a condition not far removed from actual starvation,—a fact which can neither be denied nor concealed even by the official Press.

The frightful and continually increasing misery of the toiling millions of our country is the most terrible count in the indictment against the Russian Government, and the paramount cause and justification of the rebellion against it. It would be a gross injustice to affirm that the

Government has directly ruined or purposely injured the peasantry. Why should it act with such foolish and wanton wickedness? We can well understand that a despotic Government, caring only for its own selfish interests, should object to the commonalty being educated. But it is to the Government's own material advantage to have well-to-do tax-payers rather than the beggarly ones it has now. I admit willingly that the central Government quite sincerely intended to benefit the peasants, not only morally, but economically, by the agrarian arrangement of 1861. Still more so by that of 1866, which is better than its predecessor in every respect; the Government in the latter case not having been hampered by a desire to conform to the wishes of the nobility.

Leaving out of the question the immaterial point of intentions, I am ready to go the length of acknowledging that it would be incorrect to maintain that to the Government's unintentional blunders should be ascribed the ruin which has overtaken the peasants. The new agrarian arrangement is very unsatisfactory, and the system of taxation is simply monstrous. I shall presently show how far both these elements contributed towards reducing the peasants to their present condition. But still it was not the Government's direct doing. There is one consideration which clearly proves this. Since the Emancipation the yield from the direct taxes imposed on the peasants has increased. But until 1879 their burdens had increased twelve per cent. only. Since that time they have remained stationary, and of late years there is even a slight decrease in the direct taxes—very slight, yet still a decrease. As to the impoverishment of the masses, measured by the reduced consumption of food and the increase in the rate of mortality, it is frightful and intense, and shows no sign of abatement whatever. This is proof to demonstration that there must be at work another corrosive influence more inexorable and fatal and less under control even than the actions of the uncontrollable bureaucracy.

This influence lies in the new economical system, quite opposed to the traditions and ideals of the Russian peasantry, and which has been forced on them by the Act of Emancipation. In these few pages I purpose to present a brief, yet as far as possible complete, account of the results of the Russian agrarian experiment, derived from the numerous and painstaking reports on the subject in which modern Russian literature is so rich.

But what constitutes the basis of the traditional economic conceptions of our agricultural classes? The communal system of land tenure, the reader may suggest, is its most original and striking feature. On this, however, I shall not dwell. First, because it was affected but slightly by the Emancipation Act of 1861, which gave each village commune the option either of breaking up their land into private allotments and distributing it among independent families, or keeping it as common property. Secondly, because the communal land tenure, though accepted by seventy-three per cent. of our peasantry, is only exceptional among the Ruthenians, who form the remainder of our rural population. The evil inflicted by the Emancipation Act is of a much wider reach and greater importance; it arises not from the way in which occupying owners divide their properties among themselves, but from the fact that they are fast being divorced from the soil which they till.

The Russian popular conceptions of land tenure, though they may seem somewhat heterodox to a Western lawyer or modern economist, are exactly the same as those which in past times prevailed among all European nations before they happened to fall victims to somebody's conquest. Russian peasants hold that land, being an article of universal need, made by nobody, ought not to become property in the usual sense of the word. It naturally belongs to, or, more exactly, it should remain in the undisturbed possession of, those by whom, for the time being, it is cultivated. If the husbandman discontinues the cultivation of his holding he has no more right over it than the fisher over the sea where he has fished, or the shepherd over the meadow where he has once pastured his flock.

This does not, however, imply any question as to the right of the worker over the product of his labour. In Russia a peasant who has improved and brought under tillage new land always obtains from the *mir* a right of undisturbed possession for a number of years, varying in its *maximum*, in divers provinces, from twelve to forty years, but strictly conforming in each case to the amount of labour which had been bestowed on it by the peasant and his family. During this period the occupier possesses the full right of alienating his holding by gift or sale.

But when the husbandman is supposed to have been fully remunerated for his work, all personal prescriptive right ceases.

These notions cannot be called exclusively Russian. They are deeply rooted throughout the Slavonic world, save among the few tribes who have been long subjected to Western influences and overdrilled by the feudal *régime*. The Turkish domination proved in this respect much more tolerant. The customs which prevail among the Balkan slavs are almost identical with those commonly accepted in Russia. Here, according to Bohishitch, the people do not recognize a right of property in virgin land. When cultivated, it becomes the rightful property of its occupier, and remains his so long as he continues to improve it with the work of his own hands. A tenant who has cultivated for ten years without interruption another man's land becomes *ipso facto* its legitimate proprietor and ceases to pay rent, on the ground that he has bought up, by his ten years' payments, the claims which the former landlord might have acquired. In Bulgaria, according to the same authority, the principle is pushed still further. Here simple wage labourers acquire the right of ownership over the land on which they have been employed without interruption for the ten years' period, so that farmers, in order to avoid being expropriated, change their labourers at least once before the expiration of every ten years.

In Russia, until its close alliance with Western countries in Peter the Great's time, the popular notions as to land tenure were common to all classes, the Government included. "There is no country," says Prince Wassiltchikoff, in concluding his careful study of the history of our agrarian legislation, "in which the idea of property in land was so vague and unsteady as it was until very recently with us, not only in the minds of the peasants, but also of the representatives and heads of the State. The right of use, of possession, of the occupation of land has, on the contrary, been very clearly and firmly understood and determined from time immemorial. The very word 'property,' as applied to land, hardly existed in ancient Russia. No equivalent to this neologism is to be found in old archives, charters, or patents. On the other hand, we meet at every step with rights acquired by use and occupation. The land is recognized as being the natural possession of the husbandman, the fisher, or the hunter, of him who 'sits upon it.'" In the living language of peasants of modern times, there is no term which expresses the idea of property over the land in the usual sense of the word. The expression "our land" in the mouth of a peasant includes indiscriminately the whole land he occupies for the time being, the land which is his private property (under recent legislation), the land held in common by the village (which is, therefore, only in the temporary possession of each household), and also the land rented by the village from neighbouring landlords. Here we see once more the fact of working the land identified with rights of ownership.

When serfdom was introduced, and one half of the arable land, with the twenty-three millions of human beings who lived thereon, gradually became the property of the nobility, the newly enslaved peasants found less difficulty in realizing the fact of their slavery than in understanding the law which allotted the land to those by whom it was not tilled. "We are yours," they said to their masters, "but the land is ours." "*My vashi, zemlia nasha,*"—this stereotyped, hundred times quoted phrase, vividly sums up the Russian peasant's conception of serfdom.

When, after so many years of expectation, disappointment, and delusive hopes, the longed-for day of emancipation came for the down-trodden serfs, the idea of the impending enfranchisement assumed in the rural mind only one and the same shape through all the empire—that when once restored to freedom they would not be despoiled of that which they had possessed as slaves—their land. The universal expectation, as proved by the universal disappointment, was that the freed peasants would have all the land which they had previously tilled. As to the nobles, their former masters, the Czar would keep them, they thought, henceforward "on salary, as he kept his generals." This was the ingenuous and naïve expression of a very clear and practical idea—that of the State buying out the landlords by means of a vast financial operation. This was precisely the measure advocated by Tchernyshevszy and the *Sovremennik* party as the best and most convenient solution of the Russian agrarian problem.

The Government, as might well be expected, was loth to adopt a course which seemed so hazardous and new. Fortunately for itself, it did not follow the opposite course, which would have been the signal for a tremendous popular rising—the enfranchisement of the peasants without any land at all, as suggested by the reactionary anti-abolitionist party. The freed peasants were endowed with small parcels of land, carved out of the estates of their masters, who retained, however, the greater part of their properties. The idea of the Government was to keep up the system of great landlords, while creating around them a class of resident owners.

This may have seemed a fair compromise, but in reality it was not so. In the preamble of the Emancipation Act the intention of the Government was clearly defined. " To provide the peasants," it ran, " with means to satisfy their needs, and enable them to meet their obligations to the State (payment of taxes), the peasants will receive in permanent possession allotments of arable land and other appendages, as shall be determined by the Act." Hence, a small proprietor, according to the Government's own definition, is a husbandman having a piece of land on which he can live, however poorly, and pay his taxes—a definition which economists will readily accept. A peasant in this position is, indeed, a regular " small proprietor," or resident owner. If, however, a man possess a patch of land of a few square yards, on which he can grow a bushel of potatoes, he is a "proprietor" all the same, but only from a juridical point of view. In the eyes of an economist he is a pure proletarian, amenable to the economical laws regulating the conditions of this and not the other class.

Now to which of these two categories do the enfranchised Russian peasants belong? Certainly not to that of small proprietors, in the economical sense. Neither are they pure proletarians. They partake of both characters, in what proportion we shall see further on. Let it here suffice to say that the land was so parsimoniously apportioned that the enfranchised peasants were utterly unable to provide themselves with the first necessaries of life. With few exceptions, the bulk of our peasantry are compelled to look to wage labour, mostly agricultural, on their former masters' estates and elsewhere, as an essential, and often the chief, source of their livelihood.

Thus, the Act of Emancipation did not, as its promoters intended, create side by side small and large landowners who could live and labour and thrive independently, without obstructing and damaging each other's work. The peasants were not independent of the landlords. The landlords were not independent of the peasants. There existed in Russia at the time of the Emancipation no agrarian proletariat whatever. The landlords could nowhere find regular wage labourers by whom they might replace their enfranchised serfs. The cultivation of the landlords' vast estates had either to be entirely dropped or their serfs compelled to till them for hire.

This was the new principle on which Russian rural economy had thenceforward to be based. It was decidedly opposed to our national and inveterate traditions, as I have just shown. It was borrowed from Western countries. I do not say that it was not better than serfdom. It certainly was better. Neither do I affirm that those who introduced it had the slightest suspicion of the havoc which in one generation it was destined to produce. I am simply stating a sad but undeniable fact. In social and political life, as well as in the domain of art and fiction, imitations seem always to bear the same original sin : while reproducing with great fidelity the drawbacks, imitators ignore and forget the merits of their exemplars. Thus the Capitalist order came to us without any of the free elements of polity which were its outcome in the countries of its birth. All the advantages in the impending struggle were therefore on one side. The masses were left with no means of defence, and the Government threw the enormous weight of its material and political power into the scale of wealth and against labour. The victory of the protected few over the helpless many was thenceforth assured. It was also complete and frightfully rapid.

In the following chapters I propose to describe the ways and means whereby this victory has been gained and the consequences which it has entailed. As yet Russia is an enormous, albeit a comparatively simple, economical organism. Through the puzzling and disorderly complication of private economical operations we shall discover a striking unity of cause. It is a huge economical mechanism, combined upon one leading principle and having one consistent end. I shall begin by describing its central organs, those which impart movement and life to the whole,—the banking and credit system, circulation of money, and the rest.

CHAPTER II.

For obtaining full control of the resources of the country, Russian capitalists made use of two seemingly innocent means—the railways and credit. The construction of the railways was undertaken in the first instance by the Government itself. Very soon, however, the business was transferred to private companies, which the State supplied with capital, since at that time no private enterprise could raise such enormous sums as were involved in the construction of the railways. Up to January 1883, 13,500 miles of permanent way had been laid in Russia proper, and the total amount of shares issued by the various companies was 2,210,000,000 roubles (about £22,000,000 sterling). Of this sum the Government supplied directly fifty-four per cent. —*i.e.*, more than half—the money being raised by several loans, chiefly foreign, the interest of which (four, four and a half, and five per cent.) is, of course, debited to the railway companies in their accounts with the State. In order to enable the companies to raise the remaining forty-six per cent. the Government guaranteed a *minimum* revenue, and undertook to make good out of the public funds any deficit that might arise. Nor is this all; in cases of emergency the Government still continues to make supplementary grants to these companies, which have already been so generously subsidized from the national exchequer.

With the public finances always in an unsatisfactory condition, this lavishness must needs be a grievous burden on the budget. In 1869 the national debt amounted to 1,907·5 millions of roubles, of which only 10·6 per cent. fell to the share of the railways. In January 1883 the national debt had increased to 3,267 millions of roubles, of which fully 28·3 per cent. had been contracted for the construction of railways. Thus the railway debt increased in this period absolutely fivefold, and at three times the rate of the national debt itself.

These outlays, it is true, figure in the budget as debts owing by the railway companies to the State—temporary loans which in due time will be repaid to the exchequer. But this is a mere fiction. The indebtedness of the railways to the State is continually increasing in each category under which the advances are made—viz., direct subsidies, guarantees, and interest on obligations. In 1877 the deficit in the annual payment due from the railways to the State amounted to 450·5 millions of roubles, while those of all the other debtors of the State (the peasants included) totaled up to only 154·7 millions, the railway companies thus engrossing seventy-four per cent. of the famous "arrears" (*nedoimki*) which are the plague of our finances. In the following year the railway debts had increased to seventy-seven per cent. of the total arrears, and rose subsequently to eighty per cent. In 1884 the total amount of railway debts was stated to be 886,000,000 roubles. In reality, however, it was more, because the Ministry passed a resolution to strike out of the list forty millions as "perfectly hopeless." Thus the total of railway debts in 1884 was about one and a-half times as much as the entire revenue of the State (Russian Almanac, 1886, p. 192).

It might appear from this that the railways are the most disastrous of the many ruinous Russian State enterprises, and that the companies are running the country towards the verge of bankruptcy. In reality, however, it is not so. The prospects of the railways are as bright as anything can be in Russia. The railways are, on the whole, very prosperous. They are extending rapidly, and the profits of the companies are increasing both absolutely and as compared with former years. In the period from 1870 to 1877 each mile earned in gross receipts on an average fourteen per cent. more than in the preceding period. The expenses having in the same time augmented considerably, the net increase is not so great, being three per cent. per mile. In the following five years the increase of the gross receipts was ten per cent. for each mile. The dividends received by the shareholders in 1870 amounted to 32·5 millions of roubles; in 1877 they were 71·7 millions, an increase of 2·5. Nevertheless, the indebtedness of the railways to the State shows for the same period an increase of one hundred and fifty per cent.

This seems contradictory and rather puzzling. The explanation of the riddle is, however, very simple. The various railway lines are not equally profitable, and the Government, while leaving the extra profits of the best lines to their respective shareholders, has to make up the deficiency of the remainder.

It comes practically to this:—The State, which

has supplied the railway companies either directly or indirectly with all their funds, surrenders the profits of the enterprise to individual capitalists, taking for itself only the losses. In other words, the peasants (for as they contribute eighty-three per cent. of the whole budget they are the real paymasters) are paying a group of individual capitalists a tribute amounting from 1878 to 1882 to an average of forty-six millions of roubles a year.

Let us now ascertain what are the normal use and functions of this network of railways so dearly bought by the peasants. The railways transport freight and passengers, and statistics show that in Russia both are chiefly of rural origin.

The passengers first. We have to observe before anything else that passengers of the third class make eighty-three per cent. of the whole and pay sixty-seven per cent. of all the receipts for fares. Thus even here, as everywhere else, the peasant is the main prop of the business. Why do our peasants travel so much? Not, of course, for pleasure or for health, but in search of work. The traffic returns are very significant as to the extent to which the receipts are derived from the agricultural classes. During the winter months the passenger traffic is at its lowest ebb.

In March, when field labour begins in the vast southern region of the empire, we observe, on the other hand, a sudden increase of 19·5 per cent. In April, when field labour extends to the central zones, there is a still greater increase—twenty-four per cent. over the previous month. In the following months the increase continues, though less rapidly ; the workers are at their posts busy with their work. In August the number of passengers attains its *maximum ;* the workers have done, and return after the harvest to their homes, in a body. In September the passenger traffic drops suddenly to 33·74 per cent., and goes on decreasing until the following March.

The passenger traffic, in fact, corresponds with the cycle of agricultural work. It is represented by a single wave, having its greatest amplitude in the autumn and its lowest in the winter. This is an indirect but striking confirmation of Mr. Tchaslavsky's calculations that even in the outdoor employment of our peasantry the agricultural branch has an overwhelming preponderance over the industrial.

The fluctuations in the passenger traffic show that they are the natural corollary of the periodical migrations of the tillers of the soil. The month of August, when the workers are returning wholesale to their penates, leaving behind them the produce they have harvested, presents, as we have seen, the greatest amplitude of the migratory wave. The same month gives the lowest returns for heavy freights carried at low speeds. Time is required for the collection of the produce by the hands which forward it to its destination. But in September the heavy traffic returns show a rise of 19·46 per cent., and the rise continues in October. But in November there is a sudden drop of 20·5 per cent. What does it mean? The hard winter has frozen the rivers, thus hindering the carriage of corn and other agricultural products to the railway stations by water, the usual method, the transport by horses and oxen and carriages being too expensive. During the winter months there is little shipping of produce. But in March, when the rivers of the southern provinces are reopened to navigation, traffic increases 14·57 per cent. In May, when the navigation is open throughout Russia, the increase is 40·27 per cent., the same high rate being maintained in June. The pressure is then over, heavy traffic diminishes, and the diminution goes on until the following September. Goods traffic, in fact, like the passenger traffic, corresponds with the cycle of the agricultural year, with this difference—that while the shipping of merchandise, owing to climatic conditions, is divided into two pulsations, the movement of passengers has but one.

Now let us consider the other part of the mechanism—first, the all-powerful agent which sets in motion all this vast machinery—money. Ordinary banks were first introduced into Russia in 1864. Before that time the "Bank of the State"—the official bank of the Empire—was practically the sole institution of the sort in Russia. In 1864 its capital amounted to fifteen millions of roubles, with 262·7 millions of private deposits. Of this sum forty-two millions only were used for commercial purposes by way of advances on mercantile paper. In 1877 the capital of all the banks amounted to 167·8 millions, the deposits to 707·5 millions of roubles. In these thirteen years banking capital was increased more than eleven-fold, and the deposits more than three-fold ($3\frac{1}{4}$). At the same time the method of employing banking capital underwent a thorough change. In 1864 only fifteen per cent. of the capital was, as we have seen, employed in discounts. In 1877 almost the whole—ninety-six per cent.—was used in this way. Loans and discounts for business purposes show a still more rapid increase. From 23·7 millions in 1864 the bills under discount rose to five hundred millions of roubles, more than twenty-one times as much. With the enormous increase in banking capital the rapidity of its circulation has moreover doubled. In 1863 the entire deposits were turned over about twice in a twelvemonth (1·85). Thirteen years later they were turned over nearly five times in the same period.

The increase of money power has been enormous, the progress of commerce almost febrile in its intensity. Now, what are its objects and character? Banking statistics give a peremptory answer. Its chief object is the manipulation of raw agricultural produce.

It must be observed, by way of explanation, that, notwithstanding the great development of banking facilities, the vast majority of commercial transactions are settled with ready money. According to the accounts of the Bank of the State, of all the bills discounted by the Bank and its branches only fourteen per cent. are not liquidated where they are drawn. The ready money thus obtained is used for the payment for grain and other produce.

Let us examine how this transfer of money varies during the year. The circulation of money is at its lowest ebb twice a year. Its active period begins about the end of harvest time, in July; but very slowly at first, the rise being only 1·06 per cent. In August it makes a sudden leap of 19·31 per cent. In September the increase is still greater—38·03 per cent.—and it remains at the same figure during October. November is marked by a decrease of 46·44 per cent., and at this level it remains until February. Then in the spring it begins to rise once more, showing in May a total incease of 47·8 per cent. Thus the double pulsation of money exactly corresponds with the fluctuations of railway traffic receipts, which, as we have seen, are at their highest in September and May. In the centre of our financial system, St. Petersburg, the streaming out of money somewhat precedes the influx of corn. The money which leaves St. Petersburg accumulates for a short time in the provincial banks, whence it flows to the various local corn markets, where the produce is stored in September and in May.

The two waves which represent the yearly pulsation of money—the autumn wave and the spring wave—though quite similar as to their exterior form, differ greatly as to their object and significance.

The produce sold in the spring is that of the previous year, which, owing to the freezing of the rivers, could not be moved sooner. The money remitted from the centres to the provinces during the spring season is used solely for speculative purposes. The grain passes from one buyer to another, and capitalists now begin to struggle among themselves.

The September circulation of money is of quite a different nature. It signifies that the capitalists are coming into direct contact with the producers. Now not only the corn stores but the granaries of the millions of peasants are filled with as much grain as they are allowed by the fates to possess. The smallest village becomes during this season a little corn market. The quantity of potential bread which the farmer sells or keeps for his own consumption is not yet settled, his need of money contending with his desire for food. The greater the amount of money thrown on the market the greater will be the victory of the capitalist over the producer. The capitalists, therefore, strain every nerve to have the best of the battle. The cash reserves of the banks—State as well as private—are heavily drawn upon. Private deposits are also utilized for the same purpose. The September deposits sink to 0·35 per cent. of their yearly average. All the disposable capital of the Empire finds its way into the hands of the corn merchants, whose agents traverse the country far and wide, doing their utmost to obtain from the peasants as much of their yearly harvest, and leave them as little, as they can, because it is on the success of these operations that depends their profit for the year.

Finally, in this critical moment of the struggle between the purses of the merchants and the stomachs of the peasants, the State intervenes in favour of capital by making a new issue of paper money.

It must be remembered that in Russia, "money," so far as interior markets are concerned, means exclusively paper money. Silver and copper coin is used for small change only. Commercial transactions are carried on by " credit roubles," which are nominally convertible into gold and silver, but in reality are not convertible at all, but only saleable at their effective value, which fluctuates between sixty and sixty-five per cent. of their nominal value.

The abuse of this privilege of issuing paper money is one of the many causes of the miserable condition of our finances. But in the regular course of affairs this potent means of influencing the market is altogether subservient to the interests of the capitalists.

Paper money is subject during the year to a double process—the periodical issues and withdrawals, apart from the mere substitution of new for worn notes. The regular issues (omitting exceptional cases) begin at the end of summer, "to reinforce the branches," precisely when the money begins to stream rapidly from St. Petersburg to the provinces. The issues are increased as the demand for money increases on the corn market. In July it is twenty-one per cent. of the whole yearly issue, in August nine per cent.; in September, when the demand reaches fever heat, 56·54 per cent.—that is to say, more than one-half of the whole issue for the remainder of the year. And in the three months of the autumn market season the Exchequer issues eighty-six per cent. of the paper money of the year, whereby is caused a depreciation of the credit rouble, which in this season can be obtained at its lowest price both in the world's money markets and in all Russian financial centres. But the cost of the operation is borne by the *moujiks*. The wave of depreciation of the paper rouble does not reach the green fields of Russia, the villages and hamlets where the bargain is struck. Here the enormous mass of paper money advanced by the State and the banks to the traders keeps all its buying power, and takes from the producers the corresponding quantity of their produce.

The peasants receive the money. The autumn is the only time of the year when they have the pleasure of holding in their hands the yellow, green, and blue painted strips of paper called money. But they do not keep it long—just long enough to dirty it. They return it faithfully in the form of taxes to the State, in order that it may next year repeat the same operation with the same results. Paper money returns to the Exchequer, which can then proceed to withdraw it from circulation. This operation is effected chiefly during the winter season, the old paper money being burnt in a furnace in the courtyard of the " Bank of the State," to the great consternation and excitement of the St. Petersburg roughs, who always gather round to stare at such a strange and incomprehensible spectacle.

This brief and dry sketch shows clearly that the whole economical life of this colossal Empire —railways, banks, finances—so far as interior policy goes, is concerned with the manipulation of the agricultural produce, which, ready in August, is sold in September, and carried by the railways in the autumn and the following spring.

It remains only to indicate the end and result of this comprehensive operation. Whither is all this grain conveyed? To the great foreign markets, in order to extract from them as much gold as they can be made to yield. The interior exchange has no interest for us, since produce and money alike remain in the country.

The export of Russian corn since the Emancipation has increased with wonderful rapidity. In 1860-4 we exported nine million quarters. In the following five years the export increased to ten millions, then to twenty-one millions, and finally, 1875-79, reached its highest point—an average of thirty-three millions. The following five years, 1880-85, exhibit a sudden stoppage to this rapid progress. The export is maintained at the same high standard of thirty-three millions a year without any further increase. We shall presently see the real significance of this ominous hitch. Still on the whole things seem to be very satisfactory. In a score of years the value of our corn exports increased sevenfold, and became the leading article of our foreign trade, the proportion being sixty-two per cent., as compared with thirty-three per cent. in previous years. In the three triennial periods from 1870 to 1879, the taxes were increased—first 6·24 per cent., then 3·89, and finally 3·69 per cent. It shows that the State, on its part, took care to profit by this apparent prosperity. As for the capitalists, they are simply rolling in wealth. In the same period their profits, as shown by the sums deposited by them in the banks, increased thirty-three per cent., then thirty-eight per cent., and finally fifty per cent. It looks splendid!

The fact which puts this capitalist splendour in quite another light is that, according to official statistics, our agriculture for the last fifteen years has been in a state of almost utter stagnation. There is a wide difference, of course, between the harvests of two consecutive years, the *minimum* (1876) being 156¼ millions of quarters, the *m*ᴏₓt.

mum 231¾ millions, or forty-two per cent. more. But if we divide the period 1871-1882 into three periods, the fluctuations are seen to be insignificant (1·80 per cent.)—in point of fact, *nil*. As, moreover, in this time the quantity of corn sown increased 2·1 per cent., it results that the productiveness of agriculture even slightly diminished (0·3 per cent.). The growth of our foreign corn trade has, therefore, been forced to the detriment of the people. It has lessened the quantity of bread left for their maintenance. The population in the meantime has continually increased. In the absence of additional supplies of bread the new-comers must take what they require from the share of their elders. By comparing the increase of the population (six per cent.) with the increase of the corn export, we find that the cereal food supply available for our peasant families has fallen off on an average fourteen per cent. In other words, a Russian peasant consumes one-seventh less bread than he did fifteen years ago. Nor is this all. His food, besides being diminished in quantity, has deteriorated in quality. The best wheat (seventy-eight per cent. of the entire crop) is naturally chosen for export. Practically this means the whole, as something must needs be left for seed and the consumption of the well-to-do. The wheat flour once used by the peasants on holidays and for their children's food they can no longer afford. And now rye, their daily bread, and the oats which they require for their cattle, are also becoming large articles of export.

It has fared no better with the live stock, which form the peasants' working power and occasional food. From 1864 to 1883 the export of cattle increased thirteen-fold, with the result that cattle have greatly diminished in number in all the provinces of Russia Proper, to the great injury both of the health of the people and the productiveness of the soil.

Thus the whole economical arrangement is doing its part admirably. All the parts of the colossal machine work into one another like the toothed wheels in clock-work. Its mainspring, which imparts life and activity to the whole concern, is money, or, to be exact, the inconvertible paper money issued by the State and put into circulation by the banks. Paper money has been issued by the Government in such enormous quantities that the credit rouble, always falling, lost between 1864 and 1882 twenty-nine per cent.

of its buying power in the world's markets. Yet in the interior markets, especially in the villages, it has hardly depreciated at all. We are without statistics as to the prices at which corn is bought from the peasants in their own villages by the local or travelling agents of capitalists. It is doubtful whether we shall for a long time have such statistics, owing to the character of the transactions in question, concerning which I shall say something further on. The only figures we possess refer to the prices in the markets whither the corn is conveyed after being bought from the peasants.

Now, these prices, which are obviously higher than those ruling in the smaller markets, show a rise, it is true, but only about a third of what it should be as compared with the depreciation of the credit rouble, which points to the conclusion that in the interior of Russia the average value of corn has undergone little, if any, change. This is the *crux* of the question. The enormous issues of paper money have so augmented the buying power of capitalists as to give them more and more the control of agricultural produce, a result to which the action of the banks has largely contributed, chiefly by stimulating the circulation of capital. In the fourteen years' period during which the State increased the mass of paper money thirty-one per cent., the turnover of the banks increased by nearly seventy per cent. They have thus done twice as much for capitalists as the Exchequer has done, for by halving the time during which each rouble formerly lay dormant they have doubled its effective power. As the use of cheques and clearing offices is rapidly extending, this process is likely to be carried still further. The banks, moreover, now absorb much of the floating capital of the country, the greater part of which is placed at the disposal of corn factors exactly at the time when they are doing their utmost to take from the impoverished peasant all the produce he can be induced to sell.

The railway network, which, from nine hundred and ninety-three miles at the time of Emancipation extended in the following twenty-two years to 16,155 miles (for the whole Empire), and is still extending at the rate of about eight hundred miles each year, serves to widen and extend this activity over new districts and provinces, the chief work of the railways being, as we have seen, the transport of agricultural products and agricultural producers.

All is well combined, and the whole acts like a colossal hydraulic press, which squeezes from the peasants an ever-increasing part of their daily bread. In about fifteen years it has squeezed from them just one-seventh. From manuals of political economy we learn that when the supply of corn is diminished to the extent of a sixth of its ordinary amount the value of it rises to famine rates. Russian peasants are, however, unable to obtain higher prices; for the want of merchandize on the one hand, and possession of money on the other, are the sole factors which influence the markets. The fact remains, that, as the peasants have been compelled to sacrifice a seventh of their food supply, starvation has become their permanent condition. The economic machine has done wonders.

But how can such a miracle have come to pass? How can the peasants have been induced to give up voluntarily (because there is no compulsion on the market) that which is absolutely necessary for their own sustenance? We can well understand that a considerable rise in prices might tempt the farmers of the most prosperous country to part with a greater quantity of their produce than strict prudence would justify. But this has not been the case in Russia. The spoliation of our peasants has been effected, not by an artificial rise in prices, but simply by an increased amount of money. Every fresh issue of roubles withdraws a corresponding quantity of bread, just as a heavy body thrown into the water displaces some of the liquid. There must, therefore, be something peculiar in Russia which diminishes the usually strong natural clinging of the cultivator to the fruit of his industry, to a surprising extent. Russian peasants, who work with relentless assiduity and pluck, on the State and capitalist treadmill, would seem to have no hold whatever over the increase which the earth yields to their labour and presumably for their advantage.

To account for such a strange state of things we must leave the higher spheres of political economy and administrative mechanism and observe what may be described as the molecular action of the system. We must descend to a Russian village, such as it has become since the Emancipation, and look into the normal economy of the peasant households of which it is composed.

CHAPTER III.

RUSSIAN peasants, as I have shown, cannot be regarded as ordinary resident owners, and herein lies the gist of our agrarian question. Let us consider more closely the how and the why of this important fact.

Serfdom, as established in Russia by law and custom, took, in the regions where it struck root, a form peculiar to itself. The landlords allotted to each peasant household a certain quantity of land, and allowed them to give to its cultivation, for their own benefit, a certain proportion of their time. For the rest of their time they laboured on their master's land for his sole benefit, receiving therefor neither food nor pay. Few were the cases—when, for instance, the master was a manufacturer—where the serfs worked for him throughout the week and were boarded and lodged at his expense.

The allotment system of land prevailed everywhere, and the Government attempted to regulate the economical relations between serf and master by a law prescribing three days as the normal proportion of gratuitous work in the landlord's fields and three days in the peasant's. This law was, however, never strictly enforced. Rapacious masters could make their peasants work as long as they thought fit. Many kept the serfs four or five, some it was rumoured six days, out of the seven, leaving only Sunday for the cultivation of their own holdings. It was evident that this state of things could not last. The economical law, that the producer's remuneration cannot fall below the *minimum* necessary for keeping him alive and enabling him to rear children, operates quickly and peremptorily in every slave-owning community. The master cannot change his slaves for an equal number of fresh ones after having worn them out. The improvident *scigneur* is inevitably ruined, and stern necessity imposed the three days' rule as being the only one which sufficed to keep the human cattle in good health and strength. It prevailed generally throughout the country. The peasants gave up to their masters three days a week, or, to speak more exactly, one half of their labour (men, women, and horses), and kept the remainder for themselves.

The Emancipation Committees, in making forecasts of the proposed Act, took for their basis the existing apportionment of the peasant's time. Since there was every reason to suppose that the former masters had given to their serfs rather less land than was strictly necessary, it was at first agreed, and very wisely, that the enfranchised peasants should not be allotted smaller allotments than they had previously possessed. In carrying out the Emancipation Act this principle was, however, forgotten, altered, and mutilated. The enfranchised peasants received much less than they had previously enjoyed. I will not dwell on the legal tricks by which this purpose was effected; the clause of the *maximum* allowing the spoliation of the serfs of the smaller nobility; nor the paragraphs about "orphan shares," which permitted the creation of 700,000 downright proletarians. Neither shall I do more than allude to the blunders in the Emancipation Act concerning the pasture and forest arrangements, nor to the abuses in the settlement of agrarian matters since made by the executive, which in 1863 became decidedly reactionary, always favouring the landlords to the prejudice of their former serfs. All these details can have little interest for foreigners. Suffice it to say that the three or four dessiatines which the former serfs have on an average received, are quite inadequate to provide them with bread. In the central provinces they only have bread for two hundred days in a year, often only for one hundred and eighty, or even one hundred. The agrarian arrangement, made for the benefit of the former State peasants in 1866, was far more satisfactory than that made in connexion with the enfranchisement of the former serfs of the nobility. The State peasants were provided with twice as much land as the former serfs : a quantity sufficient on the whole to provide them with bread all the year round, supposing they had no other outgoings.

But, besides feeding themselves and their families, the peasants have to make another outlay as peremptory as eating, while possessing none of the marvellous elasticity which distinguishes human wants in general and those of Russian peasants in particular. They must pay the taxes, which, as the reader will presently learn, are rather heavy! In 1871, ten years after the Emancipation, when the first alarming symptoms of impoverishment among the peasants appeared, the Government appointed an Imperial Commission to inquire into the condition of the peasantry. These inquiries brought to light the fact that in the thirty-seven provinces of European Russia the class of former State peasants pay in taxes of every description no less than 92·75 per cent. of the average net produce of their land. As for the former serfs, being, as we have said, much worse off than their brethren, the State peasants, they have to pay a total taxation amounting on an average to 198·25 per cent. of the net produce of their land.

Thus one half of our peasantry, the former State peasants, have to give up to the State almost all that the land granted to them is capable of producing. The other moiety—the former serfs—pay away almost twice as much as the yield of their holdings. These are average figures, and, of course, not applicable to many particular cases. There are State peasants paying only from thirty to forty per cent., but there are also others who pay about one hundred and fifty per cent. (Smolensk, Kostroma, Vladimir provinces.) There are former serfs paying from seventy-six to one hundred per cent. (Petersburg province); but there are others who pay two hundred and fifty per cent. (Tver, Vladimir provinces), or three hundred per cent. (Kazan province), and more. In the province of Novgorod, according to the official statement, there is a class of peasants who pay five hundred and sixty-five per cent. (Janson, " Essay on Allotment," pp. 35, 36, and following). This will seem not merely exorbitant, but altogether absurd. How, it may be asked, can a farmer pay in taxes the whole amount or even twice or thrice as much as he gets from his land and yet live ?

The solution of the enigma lies in the smallness of the allotments. Being insufficient to furnish the peasants and their families with bread, they do not engross the whole of their working time. With our climate and our system of husbandry a peasant family, averaging seven to eight members, can cultivate fifty-four acres. Our peasants have only about a fourth of this, and the smaller their holdings the heavier relatively they are taxed. Former serfs, who spend on their diminutive allotments a fourth of their working time, and State peasants, who spend on theirs a little more than a third of their time, therefore pay to the State a half and a third respectively, because as touching the remainder of their work they are hardly taxed at all. These are heavy burdens. What would an English taxpayer say if he had to give up a third or a half of his income, however small it might be? But the thing is comprehensible and clear.

It is equally clear that our peasants, though "landed proprietors" in the eyes of the law, would not be so considered by an economist. Neither, on the other hand, could he classify them as agricultural proletarians. They stand between the two. On the average, our peasants of both classes can get from their land only about one-third of their livelihood, taxes included, hence the remaining two-thirds must be obtained by out-door work, and they are constrained to seek occupation as day labourers, home artisans, *métayers*, and so forth. They stand, in fact, one-third above the downright agrarian proletarian and two-thirds below the ordinary small resident owner.

We shall, however, fail to realize the condition of our agricultural classes if we do not take into account the fluctuations of harvests. Were harvests always the same, our peasants would have to devote to their land exactly the same amount of time every year, and every year there would be the same supply of labour in the labour market. The position would then be clear and constant for both parties—employers and employed. But it is not so in reality. Far from being constant, the harvest in Russia shows the widest fluctuations, depending, as it needs must in a country where agriculture is so primitive and backward, altogether on the caprices of nature and climate. The normal yield of grain is very low—only 2·9 for one (seed excluded) is the average for the whole Empire. But it varies greatly from year to year. In the fertile south-eastern and southern provinces, where agriculture is technically the worst, the fluctuations are the greatest. In the Middle Volga provinces in an average bad year the land yields three for one; in an average good year twelve for one; in a middling, six for one; in an exceptionally good year twenty to twenty-five for one. For Southern Russia in general the variations of the harvest are eighty-seven per cent. In the central provinces, where the system of culture is technically somewhat better, the difference between the yearly harvests is not so great, reaching, however, forty-nine, forty-seven, and twenty-one per cent. (Janson).

This state of things materially affects the mutual relations of landlords and peasants, and prevents any approach to regularity in the annual supply of labour. In an average year labourers in plenty can be obtained at average rates. In a bad year the peasants are in sore trouble and distress. They run after work in all directions and take it at starvation wages. In an exceptionally good year the position is reversed. The bulk of the peasants have plenty of work in harvesting their own crops, which they will never abandon for ordinary wages. Working on their own land they earn at the same time wages, rent, and the profit on capital. A day's labour for himself brings the peasant in as much as the wages of three days' work. So it comes to pass that there is a dearth of labour at the very moment when the landlords are most in need of hands to gather an abundant harvest. Under these circumstances it is not surprising that wages vary enormously. In bad years the wages in the Middle Volga provinces are from seventy to a hundred per cent. lower than in good years. In years of exceptional abundance wages are so high in the south-eastern provinces, the Russian granary, that it does not pay to reap the harvest unless 4,000 lbs. of wheat, or thirteen to one, are expected from a dessiatine. The field which does not promise thus much is left unharvested, and the ripe grain perishes under the burning sun.

Letting alone exceptional cases, it may be said that every change in the harvest reacts in a contrary sense, but in much greater proportion, on the prices paid for agricultural work. The widely differing condition of the peasants, consequent on the varying size of their holdings, causes every change in the harvest to throw in or out of the labour market a varying quantity of hands.

Nothing can be more absurd or disastrous for both parties and for the country in general than such a system as this. Professor Enghelhart, writing from the Smolensk province, truly observes that very high wages would be better for the landlords than these perpetual variations. A fixed rent for land and a fixed interest on capital invested in agriculture should once for all be established. As things are, every year takes its chance, and all is based on speculation. M. Giliaransky, writing about the opposite extremity of the Empire, the region of the enormous cereal plantations of the Middle Volga, comes to the same conclusion, and vividly expresses it by saying that in his country professional usurers and landlords holding 150,000 acres are the only members of the community whose solvency is not open to doubt. The smaller fry know not whether in another year they will be utterly ruined or rolling in wealth.

There could be only one issue from this indescribable economical chaos. The landlords, certainly the stronger of the two contending parties, being unable to secure a regular supply of low-priced labour by means of economic compulsion, have had to resort to a more direct and brutal form of constraint.

This they have found in the new system of bondage, or, to use the Russian word, the *kabala*, which has become an important and continually increasing influence in Russian rural life, and is in effect a simple revival, in a somewhat milder form, of the ancient serfdom.

CHAPTER IV.

THE word *kabala* is very ancient. In old annals and juridical records it was used to designate the document by which a destitute but free man sold himself to some rich man as his slave. Later on it was used colloquially to signify the state of slavery. One would have thought that after emancipation there should have been no further occasion for this ill-omened word, that it should have become obsolete. But it was not allowed to die, and is now used by Russian peasants to denote that dependency of the labourer on his employer which arises from the former's irretrievable indebtedness and impecuniosity.

That a modern Russian peasant is always liable to fall deeply into debt is unfortunately too easily demonstrated. The ordinary peasant household, taking peasants of every class, has to give up in taxes of all descriptions forty-five per cent. of its whole income (industrial work included), or in other terms about three days' work in a week. This is rather heavy, of course. The old democrat Ogareff, co-editor with Herzen of the London *Kolokol* (*Bell*), was quite right in stigmatizing the agrarian arrangement of 1861 as a new sort of serfdom, in which the State was substituted for the former *seigneurs*. Having only three days' in the week, or, what is the same, one-half of the family's working force for their own behoof, it follows that in order to make both ends meet—to live and pay taxes—the peasants must contrive never to be out of work.

Now all the employments open to them are very uncertain. The rent of land, hired from neighbouring lords for short terms, generally a year, is very heavy, owing to the fierce competition of the whole body of peasants. In the thickly-populated black earth region, the rent has risen since the Emancipation three and four fold in twenty years. On the character of the harvest depends entirely the peasants' chance of profit—if there be any. Agricultural work for wages is still more precarious. If in the far distant provinces, whither the peasants rush in swarms from the thickly-populated centres, the crops are good, the local people keep to their own fields, wages run high, the new-comers find employment readily, and return to their homes with money in their pockets. If, however, the harvest be bad they earn nothing, and have to make their way back barefoot and penniless, begging, in Christ's name, a crust of bread to keep themselves alive.

The indoor industries, in which the majority of Great Russian (Central) peasants are mostly engaged, are less remunerative than formerly, owing to the competition of the great manufactories on the one hand, and the gangrene of usury, to which all these home-working artisans are more and more exposed, on the other.

Work in manufactories is naturally the most certain. But it requires a special training, and occupies less than a million hands, one half of whom are ordinary town proletarians. Thus the economical position of our peasants is most strained and precarious. Notwithstanding their surprising industry and courage, their future is never sure. A deficit in their yearly budget is always possible, and indeed of frequent occurrence, leaving them no alternative save insolvency at the hands of the Government, or, a diminished consumption of food. These expedients, however, cannot be adopted indefinitely. The patience of tax-collectors is very short, and when exhausted is quickly followed by severe floggings and the forced sale of the insolvent's belongings.

The power of self-restraint is very great with our peasants, and the elasticity of their stomachs is simply surprising. But even these qualities have their limits. Both children and adults, when the last crust of bread is consumed, will ask for more, and the cattle, which with Russian peasants is an object of even greater solicitude than their children, cannot be left to starve. The peasant makes up his mind and looks around for some "benefactor" from whom he can borrow something.

Here we must pause. We are now at the turning-point of our social life, and the new figure which has to play the most prominent part therein is stepping on to the stage—we mean the "benefactor" or usurer. He is of two strongly marked types. The more numerous, and by far the more important of the class, socially and politically, are those who have themselves sprung from the ranks of the peasants. These are *koulaks*, or *mir*-eaters, as our people call them. They make a class apart—the aristocracy, or rather the plutocracy, of our villages. Every village commune has always three or four regular *koulaks*, as also some half-dozen smaller fry of the same kidney. The *koulaks* are peasants who, by good luck or individual ability, have saved money and raised themselves above the common herd. This done, the way to further advancement is easy and rapid. They want neither skill nor industry, only promptitude to turn to their profit the needs, the sorrows, the sufferings, and the misfortunes of others.

The great advantage the *koulaks* possess over their numerous competitors in the plundering of the peasants, lies in the fact that they are members, generally very influential members, of the village commune. This often enables them to use for their private ends the great political power which the self-governing *mir* exercises over each individual member. The distinctive characteristics of this class are very unpleasant. It is the hard, unflinching cruelty of a thoroughly uneducated man who has made his way from poverty to wealth, and has come to consider money-making, by whatever means, as the only pursuit to which a rational being should devote himself. *Koulaks*, as a rule, are by no means devoid of natural intelligence and practical good sense, and may be considered as fair samples of that rapacious and plundering stage of economic development which occupies a place analogous to that of the middle ages in political history.

The regular landlords, remnants of the old nobility, or new men, who have bought their land and stepped into their shoes, also play a very conspicuous part in the operations of rural credit, though, being total strangers in the communes, they are naturally less directly responsible for the interior decomposition of our village life. Acting as a rule through their managers and agents, who have no personal interests to serve, these large proprietors are in reality the least exacting of the gang. Yet when in difficulty the peasant will always try the *koulaks* first, who are peasants like himself. He dreads the formalities, the documents, the legal tricks and cavils which the big people have in store for a " benighted " man.

In the extensive operations of rural credit, consisting chiefly of small advances, but amounting in the aggregate to many millions of roubles yearly, the *koulaks* and rural usurers generally gain a far greater profit than do the landlords proper.

The petty capitalists who settle in the villages for business purposes, small shopkeepers, wine dealers, merchants, who always combine their special trade with more or less extensive land culture, occupy an intermediary position between that of the *koulaks* and the big landlords. They are outsiders like the latter, having by our laws no share in the administration of the commune, which is exclusively controlled by born or naturalized peasants. But by their education (or better, absence of education) and general tenor of life they are as near to the peasants as the *koulaks*, and by no means inferior to the latter in knowledge of local conditions, or in pluck, rough- ness, and cruelty.

Such are the classes who control rural credit. Whatever be its individual source in each par- ticular case, it is based on the same principle and produces the same social results. I shall therefore analyze its forms and influence cumulatively.

Regular credit—*i.e.*, advance of money to be returned in money, with the addition of interest —is very rare in our villages, unless it refers to trifling sums advanced by rural pawnbrokers. Peasants receive too little ready money to be able to depend on it for the discharge of their obliga- tions. Loans are generally made only to whole villages or to peasants' associations under the guarantee and responsibility of the *mir*. As to the interest required, and the general character of these loans, they remind us rather of Shylock's bond than of ordinary business transactions.

In January 1880, a large village of the Samara province, Soloturn, borrowed from a merchant of the name of Jaroff the sum of £600, interest being paid in advance, and bought from Jaroff's stock 15,000 puds of hay for their starving cattle. Repayment was to be made on October 1st, 1880, under the condition that £5 should be added for every day's delay. When the time of payment arrived the peasants brought £200 on account of their debt to Jaroff, who made not the slightest objection to waiting for the balance. For eleven months thereafter he kept quiet. But in September 1881 he brought an action against the village for £1,500. The magistrate before whom the case was tried, being evidently in a frame of mind not unlike that of Antonio's judges, decided against the plaintiff. But Jaroff was not much discouraged thereby. Confident in his right, he appealed to a higher court and won his case. And as this proceeding caused further delay the claim, by accumulation of interest, had doubled, and Jaroff got judgment for £3,000 in satisfaction of a debt of £600, of which £200 had been repaid! (Annals, No. 272.)

In the Novousen district of the same province the peasants of the village of Shendorf, being in great distress during the winter of 1880, borrowed from a clergyman named K—— £700, undertaking to pay him in eight months £1,050 (*i.e.*, fifty per cent. for eight months), on condition that in case of default they should give Mr. K——, pending repayment, 3,500 dessiatines of their arable land at an annual rent of ten copecks per dessiatine. As the peasants were unable to fulfil their engagement, Mr. K—— received the 3,500 dessiatines for 350 roubles, and forthwith re-let the land to the peasants themselves at the normal rent, which in this province is about five roubles (10*s.*) per dessiatine. Thus he obtained £1,715 on a capital of £700, or interest at the rate of about 250°/₀ a year. (*Idem.*)

I have quoted these examples because they possess much of what the French call *couleur locale*, and are eminently suggestive of the spirit and flavour of the financial transactions practised in our villages. They give also an idea of the great distress which prevails among peasants during the winter months, because nobody, unless on the verge of starvation, would enter into such engagements as those I have described.

The winter is, indeed, the hardest season of the year for our peasantry. The spring, too, has its difficulties, but by then field work is beginning on the neighbouring landlords' estates, and the peasants have a chance of earning a trifle. In the winter their resources are at their lowest ebb, for in September the corn was sold to pay the autumn taxes, whilst others fall due in the spring. If the household be not well off it generally has some arrears to make up, which are "flogged out" in winter. In a word, and to use their own expression, calamities beset the poor peasants from every quarter, "like snow on their heads," and they cannot avoid turning towards their "benefactors," and consenting to the most Shylockian conditions.

Regular money credit, even at the heaviest interest, is, as I have said, exceptional. Individual peasants never obtain it from a rich man, because he will not trust them without good security. Credit is mostly given on the security of the peasants' work, their hands being their most valuable possession. It assumes the form of payment in anticipation for work to be done in the next season—a sort of hypothecation of work, to be performed several months thereafter.

Agreements of this kind are always legalised at the communal offices, and often copied in their register books; it is very easy therefore to obtain a fair idea of their character. Investigators of various branches of our agrarian work have preserved for us these interesting documents.

I now have before me three such deeds—one referring to the beetroot sugar plantations of the south-west; a second to the rafting of wood and timber down the rivers, an occupation in which the peasants of the northern sylvan regions find their chief livelihood; and a third, which refers to purely agricultural work. In two the terms are almost identical, and even in the third the difference is but slight. Mr. Tchervinsky says that in his province there are special scribblers, who, having learnt the wording of these documents by heart, make their living by rewriting them for each occasion, changing only the names. Mr. Giliaransky transcribes the form of agreement for agricultural work from a *printed* original. I will give here a summary of the latter, as being the most important and characteristic, and as affording a fair idea of the others.

These agreements always begin by setting forth in great detail the work to be done, and fixing the number of dessiatines to be sown, ploughed, or harvested. Then follow a series of paragraphs intended to secure due observance of the conditions on the part of the peasant :—

"I, the undersigned, agree to submit myself to all the rules and customs in force on the estates of N. N. During the period of work I will be perfectly obedient to N. N.'s managers, and will not refuse to work at nights, not only such work as I have undertaken to do, as set forth above, but any other work that may be required of me. Moreover, I have no right to keep Sundays and holidays."

For securing good work the imposition of heavy penalties is agreed to beforehand by the subscriber, generally four or five times in excess of any damage his negligence can occasion, thereby affording a hundred pretexts for malversations, and yet quite failing in preventing the work from being on the whole very badly done.

A very important proviso remains to be noticed. The agreement never omits to mention that it retains its binding power for an indefinite number of years. Thus, if the landlord should not require his debtor to work in the immediately following summer (as might happen were the harvest deficient, and labour cheap and easily obtainable) he is free to call on him to liquidate his debt in the following year, or even the year after, thus securing for himself cheap labour at the time when wages are likely to be at their *maximum*.

The concluding paragraph is to the same effect. It states that *should the debtor be unable or unwilling to discharge his debt, or a part of it, in work, and desire to discharge it in ready money, he must pay a prescription amounting to four or five times the original loan.*

The reader will perceive that the peasants do no violence to the exact etymological value of the word in calling the winter agreement *kabala*, or bondage.

As to the purely economical side of the question —the rate of usury enforced under this system of anticipated payment of wages—we have only to compare the difference between the average wage of the labourer hired in summer and that of the unfortunates who are compelled to give themselves "in bondage" during the lean months of winter.

Here I quote a few well authenticated statements referring to the entire agricultural zone of the Empire. According to Mr. Trirogoff, the harvesting of one dessiatine in the province of Saratoff costs on an average eight roubles if carried by labourers engaged in the summer at market rates, whilst the labourer engaged in the winter receives three or four roubles for the same work. It is no uncommon thing, he adds, to see labourers of each class working side by side, the one for ten the other for three and a half roubles per dessiatine. Mr. Giliaransky states that in the Samara province the whole rotation of agricultural work for a dessiatine of land costs fifteen to twenty roubles at ordinary rates. But those labourers who are engaged in the winter are on an average only paid five roubles. In the Tamboff province, according to Mr. Ertel, free labourers receive from nine to eleven roubles, while the " bondage " (winter engaged) labourers are paid only from four to five. In the Kieff province, on the beetroot plantations, the free workers receive eight roubles and upwards for fifteen days' work, the bondage labourers only three. In the Kamenez-Podolsk province (southwest) the daily wage of free labourers is forty-five copecks in the spring and sixty copecks in summer, while the bondage labourers are paid in the same season fifteen and twenty copecks.

Thus in the Samara province the money-lenders

exact an interest equal to three hundred per cent., in Saratoff two hundred per cent., in Tamboff one hundred and eight, in Kieff one hundred and sixty-six, in the Kamenez-Podolsk two hundred per cent. on their capital, lent for a period generally not exceeding nine months.

This looks very ugly. But if the reader thinks these are exceptional extortions, of which a few greedy usurers alone are guilty, he is mistaken. There is no lack of exceptions, but they present an even blacker picture. In November and December 1881 the judge of the Valuj district (Voronej Province) had to give judgment upon forty-five suits against as many groups of peasants for failure to fulfil their engagement with their landlord J. The facts were that during the winter months of 1881 the latter advanced to the peasants of several surrounding villages a quantity of straw, wherewith to feed their cattle. The peasants had promised, as usual, to harvest for him a fixed number of dessiatines, but many—in all forty-five groups—had failed to observe the conditions agreed upon. To give an idea of these conditions I may mention that one of the groups, in a moment of sore distress, had engaged to harvest, in return for twelve cubic yards of straw advanced to them, no less than thirty-five dessiatines of corn. They harvested twenty-one dessiatines, which represented at current prices one hundred and five roubles, but being unable to harvest the remaining fourteen dessiatines they had to pay one hundred and thirty roubles more. Thus two hundred and thirty-five roubles were demanded for about five roubles' worth of straw. I leave the reader to calculate how much per cent. such usury denotes.

In the Oufa Province there are two great villages called Usman and Karmaly, with about 1,200 inhabitants. The peasants hold in common 3,890 dessiatines of land. In 1880 they borrowed from a clerk named Rvanzeff 1,019 roubles wherewith to pay their taxes. For this loan they agreed to let to him all their 3,890 dessiatines of land for three years at two roubles a dessiatine, whereas the *minimum* rent in this district is six to seven roubles. In 1881 the peasants, now left without land, rented their own holdings from Rvanzeff at seven to eight roubles a dessiatine, thus giving this gentleman a profit of 20,895 roubles, or an interest of 2,000 per cent. for the first year, and three times that amount if all the three years are taken together, on a capital of 1,019 roubles. (*Golos*, 1882, No. 113.)

Here is another instance, which is not confined to a few groups of individual peasants. In 1879, in the Province of Oufa, the whole harvest was bought from the Bashkir peasants for an advance of twenty kopecks per poud (40lb.) made during the winter. The next autumn it was resold to the same Bashkirs for one rouble twenty kopecks (120 kopecks) per poud, making an interest of 500 per cent. for about eight months.

This is really exceptional, though many pages could be filled with similar examples, which each year brings to light. It is what is called in Russia "usury." The transactions as to which I have calculated the approximate interest in various provinces are not considered usurious at all. They are only "private winter engagements," which are imposed every year on millions of peasants in every region of the empire—in the agricultural and in the industrial as well as in the sylvan. Far from considering it as something to be ashamed of, the money-lenders always pose as the peasants' " benefactors," in that they have consented to lend them money on such easy terms.

Whatever be the name we give to it, usury always remains usury, and everywhere possesses the attribute of gradually swallowing up all those who have the misfortune to step within its bounds, like a quaking bog. After discharging out of his very modest and strained resources such exorbitant claims as I have described (no matter what form the usury takes), the peasant will, generally speaking, be worse off the next autumn than he was the year before. He will have greater difficulty in defraying the taxes and in providing for his own wants. Unless unusually good luck befall him, he will be obliged during the winter to apply once more, and probably for a larger advance, to his " benefactor." Very often he will have been unable to execute all the heavy obligations previously undertaken. Some arrears will still remain to be added, with accumulated interest, to his debt of work, a debt from which he can never, except by the help of some windfall or God-send, escape.

Only very large families, which are becoming less common, are able to extricate themselves from the usurer's net in which they have been by dire misfortune entangled. When the liability is divided amongst twelve or more adults they may compensate for the absence of one or two of their number "given in bondage" by increased diligence on the part of those that remain. But small families almost inevitably succumb. Mr. Trirogoff tells us that the peasants themselves are convinced that when a man has once been caught by the rural usurer he must remain "in bondage" to the end of his days. And in nine cases out of ten this proves true.

Thus the new economical *régime* which has struck root in Russia is not only extending but acquiring a permanent force. "In the Saratoff Province whole districts are in a state of bondage" (Trirogoff). "In the Samara Province there are many villages, small and great, which have the bulk of their working strength pawned, or given in bondage, to use the peasant's expression, for many years to come, to sundry large corn growers" (Giliaransky). In the Ousman district alone (Tamboff Province), according to Mr. Ertel's very moderate estimate, the winter engagements amount to 240,000 roubles, equal to about 500,000 roubles a year at market value. There is no Province, no district, in which the system does not extensively obtain.

In some provinces it becomes from the first

a permanent bondage without the money-lender having the trouble and expense of rebinding his client every year, or of involving him in the net of accumulated interest. One of the experts for the Kherson Province made the following statement before the official inquiry commission, as registered in its official records:—"With us," he said, "there exists another mode of harvesting, extremely ruinous for the peasants. They receive from some landlord a loan of ten roubles (£1), and in return are under the obligation of harvesting, in lieu of interest, one dessiatine of corn and two dessiatines of hay, and of refunding the capital sum in the autumn. If, however, the money is not refunded, the same agreement holds good for the next year, and so on. New loans are not refused, but are made under the same conditions. Thus the peasants gradually fall into a state of bondage worse than was the old serfdom, for they are generally unable to refund the capital, and obliged to work from year to year quite gratuitously."

In the Province of Kieff yet another form of bondage obtains which approaches still more nearly the form of the old serfdom. Here the landlord advances eighteen roubles, for which sum he is entitled to receive in lieu of interest two days' work per week, *i.e.*, one hundred and four days a year. The women have to do similar slave work as interest for an advance of twelve roubles. The advance of one-half of these sums entitles the landlord to one day a week. If the peasant misses a day he is mulcted in fifty kopecks (a woman thirty-five kopecks) a day, the amount being put to his debit. When these mulcts reach the sum of nine roubles for a man and six for a woman, another day a week is added by way of interest to their debt. (*Kieff Telegraph*, 1875, No. 52.)

At this point, however, exploitation of the peasant's labours receives a self-acting check. Credit on the hypothecation of future earnings is limited by the amount of work which it is physically possible for the debtor to perform. In the fertile steppes of the south-western region, so highly favoured by nature and the Emancipation Act, which gave them the largest allotments, and in isolated districts where the peasants are exceptionally well off, the struggle between landlords and peasants has ended in the subjugation of the latter in the way I have described, but has gone no further. In all these places credit assumes chiefly the form of the hypothecation of future labour.

But in less favoured regions, and especially in the densely populated central provinces of the empire, other and more desperate and ruinous forms of credit are being developed with alarming rapidity. Potential property, labour, ceases to be a sufficient guarantee for the money-lenders. The impoverished peasants, driven to despair by famine or by fear of a forced sale of their effects, borrow money right and left, undertaking to give the lenders three times more work than they are physically able to perform. To avoid disappointment and the troubles of litigation, the usurers demand as security substantial property —the very implements of agricultural work, the cattle and the land. Both produce identical and almost equally rapid results. Deprivation of cattle and loss of land go on simultaneously.

The peasant's indispensable instruments of labour, the cattle, are sold in enormous quantities. The sales are made during the winter months and in the spring, chiefly at the time when the taxes and arrears are " flogged out." This accounts for the curious fact that in the provincial towns a pound of meat is sometimes cheaper than a pound of bread. Exports of cattle have increased for the same reason enormously; the increase since 1864 is equal to 1,335 per cent.

Statistics likewise disclose, in the thirteen Provinces of Central Russia, a decrease of 17·6 per cent. in large cattle and a reduction of 27·8 per cent. in the quantity of harvested corn, notwithstanding the increase (6·6 per cent.) of the population since 1864; the inventory of horses taken in 1882 for military purposes shows that one fourth of the peasant households no longer possess horses at all (Janson).

A peasant who has lost his cattle can no longer be considered a tiller of the soil. His imprescriptible right as the member of a village community to a share in the land becomes purely nominal and practically void. Yet, though he may give up agricultural work in his allotment, and can no onger in any way turn it to account, he still remains liable for the taxes.

Very often the peasant's road to ruin is reversed; the sale of his cattle not sufficing to meet his engagements, he is obliged to part, bit by bit, with his land. True, the laws in force do not permit peasants to sell their allotments for which the price of redemption—payment for which in most cases extends over forty-nine years from 1861—has not been provided. But the law in this regard is evaded by the expedient of long leases. The letting of land by peasants to capitalists of the upper classes—burghers, clergymen, or nobles—is exceptional. It is done wholesale by entire *mirs*, and generally for short periods. Letting to *koulaks*, or peasant capitalists, is, on the contrary, quite common and much in vogue. It is done wholesale and retail both by groups and by individual peasants. The law cannot interfere with the mutual relations of members of the same community. At the present time, the new peasant *bourgeoisie*, the *koulaks*, legally have got into their hands vast quantities of inalienable communal land under the form of long leases, which they will hold until the "next redistribution." The peasants, the nominal proprietors, work on it meanwhile as agrarian proletarians.

There are no complete estimates as to the area of land engrossed by this new rural aristocracy, but isolated inquiries in the central Provinces, where the process of social fermentation has been the most marked, prove it to be very considerable. Writing about one of the Tamboff districts, which are rather favoured by the agrarian settlement—

the Ousman district, where the majority of the population were formerly State peasants—Mr. Ertel states that in an average and rather prosperous district, which he selected for investigation, 25,258 peasants' households (one-third) pawned some of their land every year. The total area of land pawned to the *koulaks* was 8,419 dessiatines a year in the mean.

Mr. Tereshkevitch, Chairman of the Statistical Board of the Poltava Province, in a work to which was awarded the great gold medal of the St. Petersburg Geographical Society, shows that in the Poltava Province, the land of the former Cossacks, inalienable by law, is concentrated, to the extent of 24 to 32·6 per cent. of the total area, in the hands of rich *koulaks*. Here 16·5 to 29·8 per cent. of the population are downright landless proletarians. Nearly one-half (forty-three to forty-nine per cent.) have their land curtailed, sometimes to one-fourth, one-fifth, and one-sixteenth of a dessiatine; so that, according to the peasant's graphic expression, "the rain falls from your own roof on to your neighbour's land." The *koulaks*, however, who constitute 5·4 per cent. of the population, have twenty dessiatines (54 acres) and upwards per household, and among them are many who hold 100 dessiatines (270 acres), sometimes 300 dessiatines (810 acres), of the richest black soil, per household. (Report of the Geographical Society for 1885.)

Having no positive figures for the whole empire, I shall not venture to estimate, even approximately, how great a proportion of the peasants' land the *mir*-eaters, or *koulaks*, have already devoured. But we can gauge the havoc they have wrought in another way—by the number of agricultural proletarians, landless and homeless, that modern Russia possesses.

In the epoch of Emancipation Russia had no agricultural proletariat whatever. It was expected that our traditional system of land tenure, with periodical redistributions, would preserve Russia for ever from this drawback of old civilizations. Some ten years later, however, it was discovered that agrarian proletarianism had already come to be a fact. In 1871, according to the calculations of Prince Vasltchikoff, districts existed in Russia where five, ten, and even fifteen per cent. of the rural population had become downright proletarians. "Since that time" (I am quoting the words of so unimpeachable an authority as the chairman of the St. Petersburg Congress of

Russian Farmers, held on the 4th March, 1886),—
"Since that time, the agrarian proletariat has increased with alarming rapidity. From the statistical investigations of the Moscow and other *zemstvos*, we are able to affirm that the number of proletarians has increased at least from fifteen to twenty-five per cent. This shows that one-fifth of the whole population of the empire (one-third of the rural population of Russia Proper), or *about twenty millions of souls, are agrarian proletarians.* Thus the number of proletarians we have at present is equal to the number of serfs Russia possessed before the Emancipation. And I will not venture to judge how far the life of our modern agrarian proletarian is preferable to that of the former serfs."

Further on in the same speech the causes of this devastation and miserable condition of our agriculture are pointed out :—

"Thriving estates are those where the proprietors use 'bondage' (*kabala*) labour—*mir*-eaters and usurious landlords (practising the winter engagement system)—and perhaps that of peasants with large families. For all the rest, agriculture has become a risky and not very profitable business. The 'bondage' labour, which is chiefly used by the landlords, is a labour of the lowest quality, much inferior to that of the former serfs ; while the 'bondage' peasants themselves, wasting an enormous quantity of their working time on the landlords' estates, are unable to cultivate their own land even tolerably, and must drop husbandry altogether."

CHAPTER V.

THE results of emancipation, a measure from which so much was expected, must needs greatly disappoint all who are in favour of peasant ownership, especially if they have likewise put some trust in the Russian communal system of land tenure. But those who hold the opposite view will probably conclude that the process of peasant spoliation, though a painful process, and an unavoidable evil, is yet in some sort an advantage, since it may be the beginning of a new development of agriculture which will eventually put Russia on a level with Western countries and force on it the same system of land tenure.

It is quite evident that Russia is marching in this direction. If nothing happens to check or hinder the process of interior disintegration in our villages, in another generation we shall have on one side an agricultural *proletariat* of sixty to seventy millions, and on the other a few thousand landlords, mostly former *koulaks* and *mir*-eaters, in possession of all the land. When starvation has depleted the market of some ten or fifteen millions of superfluous agricultural proletarians, the landlords will doubtless introduce an improved system of agriculture of the regular European type, and the remainder of our rural population will become common wage-labourers. Then, and only then, will there begin true agricultural progress in Russia. In the present transitory stage, however, the landlord system is technically as bad as it well can be. It is chiefly based on bondage labour, which is cheaper than any other; cheaper than machinery, cheaper than that of the worst paid common labourers, who must be nourished after all at their master's expense, and get something (from £4 to £5 a year) for taxes and clothing. As to bondage labour, it can be got for next to nothing after the first payment. Then the work done merely represents the exorbitant interest on the trifling sums advanced years before, to which may have been added, out of pity, a few sums equally trifling.

But the peasant, enslaved by usury, has repaid his extortioners in another way—by the utter negligence, slovenliness, and dirtiness of his work. He is bound to labour on the landlord-creditor's land, and ostensibly conforms to the conditions of his bond. No power on earth, however, can prevent his working as hastily and as badly as he is able—from doing his "level worst," as an American would say. No amount of superintendence can compel diligence, unless, indeed, the landlord has one superintendent for every bondsman. These men cannot be terrorized and beaten into carefulness and industry as were the former serfs. On the other hand, neither is he in the least impressed, as the free wage-labourer is, by dread of dismissal. He has, in a word, no motive whatever to work well, and every reason on earth to get rid of his ungrateful task as quickly as may be. The work supplied by the bondage system is of the worst possible description. M. Gilaransky says:—

"Where the free peasants harvest five stacks, the bondage people harvest only four or three and a half. In the field you recognise at first sight the work done by bondage people and by free labourers. With the latter the freshly-mown field presents a nice, even surface, showing no trace of former vegetation, while the bondage labourers always leave long strips of grass unmown. In the fields of well-to-do peasants you will find not a handful of spikes or straw, the closely-cut stubble field extends even and uniform like a hair-brush on every side. But the fields of the big landlords, after the bondage people's harvesting, are pictures of haste and dirt. Here and there you see black spots as if swine had been grubbing; these are places where the children, in helping their elders, have uprooted the crops with their hands. Great clumps of unreaped grain are left behind, and the whole field, covered with scattered spikes and straw, seems rather creased and trampled than mown."

With such methods as these no improvement in husbandry can be thought of. Scientific culture is impossible. The cereal planters understand all this only too well, and, taking the bondage work as it is, make splendid profits by speculating on the enormous extension of tillage, thus compensating by the extent of land cultivated for the very low technical quality of the culture.

Such few estates as are in a satisfactory, sometimes even a model state of cultivation, are those where the proprietors have adopted the heroic resolution of keeping an adequate number of permanent labourers, and paying them fair wages—in other words, of investing considerable capital and getting for it small, though regular, returns. Such capitalist heroism is, however, necessarily exceptional. The great majority of capitalists find it much more advantageous to spend as little as possible on each acre, keeping only a small staff of managers on permanent wages, speculating on the extreme cheapness of labour, and avoiding the costly luxury of scientific agriculture.

The *koulaks* and *mir*-eaters, the new land forestallers of peasant origin, are in a much better position as touching bondage work than are their fellow loanmongers of the upper crust. These rural Crassuses very often wield the same influence in their diminutive village republics, as their protagonist, the famous Roman usurer, wielded in Rome, and for the same reasons; a *koulak* is not to be trifled with, and a poor peasant, his debtor, will think twice before cheating him as he would cheat a landlord. He well knows that the *koulak* will find a thousand occasions for revenge. Moreover, the *koulak* and all the members of his family work together on the same fields as their bondsmen, keeping constant watch over them.

On the whole, the *koulaks* and *mir*-eaters, as all observers agree, obtain by the bondage system tolerably good work. Working for a *koulak* exhausts the peasant's strength, while work on a landlord's estate is little more than a waste of time. Employing a much greater proportion of bondage work relatively to their capital than the regular landlords, and possessing the above-mentioned advantages, the *koulaks* and *mir*-eaters grow in numbers, riches, and power with startling rapidity. But being in so advantageous a position, the *koulaks* have even less inducement than the regular landlords to change their tactics and waste money on any permanent improvements. So long as there is a crowd of people on whom they can impose their yoke so cheaply and easily, their culture will continue to be as loose and predatory as it has hitherto been; only, instead of exhausting the land, as the regular landlords are doing, they are exhausting the labourer.

Thus the concentration of land in the hands of individual proprietors has imparted, as yet, neither order nor progress to our agriculture. The process of land concentration, if not stopped, will, doubtless, achieve in time both these results, but in another way—by starving out an adequate part of our rural population. It may be added that this charitable work is going on with the greatest success. I will not go into details, neither will I harrow the reader by sensational pictures. I shall only quote figures, some statistical, which speak for themselves.

The rate of mortality in the whole of Russia is very high, fluctuating between 35·4 and 37·3 per thousand. Taking thirty-six as the mean, we find that in Russia, with its thin population and a climate as healthy as that of Norway and Sweden, the mortality is one hundred per cent. greater than in the latter, and one hundred and twelve per cent. greater than in the former of those countries. It is sixty-four per cent. greater than in Great Britain; thirty-seven per cent. greater than in Germany; and thirty-nine per cent. greater than in France.

According to Dr. Farr, a mortality exceeding seventeen per thousand is an abnormal mortality, due to some preventable cause. This standard is reached in Norway, and approached very nearly in Sweden, and in the rural districts of England (where it is eighteen per thousand), and even in several large centres of population in the United States. In England, whenever the death-rate rises to twenty-three per thousand a medical and sanitary inquiry of the district is prescribed by law, this mortality being considered due to some preventable cause. It cannot be otherwise in Russia with a death-rate of between 35·4 and 37·3. And it is not at all difficult to discover that this preventable cause lies in the misery of the unhappy country. The Congress of the Society of Russian Surgeons expressed exactly the same opinion at their last annual meeting, held on the 18th of December, 1885, under the presidency of M. S. P. Botkin, body-surgeon to the Emperor. After ascertaining the exact death-rate, they expressed the opinion that the primary cause of this frightful mortality is deficiency of food (bread). It is thus obvious that the reduction of one-seventh in the peasants' consumption of bread during the last twenty years, as is shown by the computation of corn exports and corn production, has not come out of the people's superfluities, but is literally wrung from their necessities.

The Congress of Russian Surgeons of December 1885 brought to light some other very suggestive facts. This high rate of mortality is not uniform throughout the Empire; it is much greater in its central than in its peripheral regions. The high birth-rate in Russia, due to the very early marriages of our agricultural population, atones in part for the devastation produced by untimely deaths. Statistics show an average yearly increase of 1·1 per cent. (or about 1,200,000) in the number of the unfortunate subjects of the Czar. But there is no such increase in the central provinces, where the population is more dense, and the ruin of the masses proceeds with the greatest rapidity.

In the thirteen provinces—that is to say, the whole of Central Russia—the mortality, always on the increase, reached when the last census was taken (1882) *sixty-two per thousand per annum.* Nothing approaching this prevails in any other part of Europe. It would be incredible were it not officially attested. The birth-rate in these provinces being forty-five (the normal rate for the whole Empire), this is equal to a decrease of seventeen per thousand per year. In the heart of Russia the population is being starved out.

The medical report, moreover, notices that the provinces where the mortality is greatest are those where the land produces a full supply of bread. The starving out of the peasants who till it is, therefore, the work of "art," as I have just described, and not of nature.

Another most suggestive fact which points to the same conclusion is that Russia is the only country in the world where the mortality over a large area of open country is greater than that in the towns. In all countries possessing statistical records it is the reverse, the hygienic conditions of life and work in the open air being all in favour of the rural population. In England, for instance, the mortality is 38·8 per cent. higher in towns than in the country; in France, twenty-four per cent; and in Sweden, thirty-seven per cent. In Prussia the difference is less than in any other part of Western Europe—7·1 per cent.; yet even there it is in favour of the villages. In Russia there are fourteen provinces, with a population as great as that of the Austrian Empire, and an area three times as large, in which the death-rate of the villages is higher than that of the largest towns. In the villages of the province of Moscow, the mortality is 33·1 higher than in Moscow city; in the province of St. Petersburg the difference is 17·5; in Kazan and Kieff, with more than 100,000 inhabitants each, the mortality is less by twenty-seven and thirty per cent. than in the villages of their respective provinces (Professor Janson's Statistics, Vol. I., p. 264).

I hardly need to add that such a striking anomaly can in nowise be put to the credit of the exceptional perfection of the hygienic arrangements of our big cities. The largest, the two capitals included, are in this respect much more nearly allied to Asiatic than to European towns.

Another startling fact is, that the official returns relating to recruits for the period from 1874 to 1887, published in 1886 by the central Statistical Board, show that the number of able-bodied young men decreases every year with appalling regularity. In 1874, when the law of universal military service was for the first time put in action, out of the total number of young people tested by the recruiting commissioners seventy and a half per cent. were accepted as ablebodied. The next year showed even a somewhat higher rate—seventy-one and a half per cent. of able-bodied. But since that date the decrease has gone on uninterruptedly. It was 69·4 in 1876. Then 69, 68·8, 67·8, 67·7, 65·8, 59·1, and finally, in 1883, fifty-nine per cent. This means a decrease of twelve and a half per cent. in nine years in the number of able-bodied people among the flower of the nation, that is, the youth of twenty years of age, of whom eighty-five and a quarter per cent. come from the peasantry.

These facts need no comment. They admit of only one explanation; hunger and poverty have wrought fearful havoc among our rural population. This is the last work of our present *régime*. It is to this we have come after twenty-five years of incessant "progress," and the worst of it all is, that under the present *régime* the work of ruin and devastation must go on uninterruptedly, fatally, rather increasing in its rapidity than diminishing.

For what are the chief causes of peasant degradation? Usury on the one hand and taxes on the other. The first of these causes, in the material ills which it produces, is by far the more powerful and fatal of the two. But the *koulaks*, *mir*-eaters, and usurers of all sorts would never have been able to lay hold of and re-enslave the recently enfranchised agrarian population without the aid of the tax-gatherer and his satellities. What is it that constrains the peasants to sell in September corn which they know they will be in desperate need of a few months later on? The imperious necessity of paying their taxes.

The ideal of each peasant's household is to eat the bread from their own fields, providing for the taxes by outdoor work or by some home industry. But few are able to realize their ideal. The vast majority, as I have already shown, sell a considerable proportion of their harvest in September, only to buy it back in the winter or the spring, always losing heavily thereby, because corn is cheap in September and from thirty to fifty per cent. dearer in the winter and spring. Nevertheless they commit each year this economical absurdity, which they thoroughly understand. They risk hunger, knowing well how hard it is to make money in winter. They are aware that in such cases they will have no other resource than to "give themselves in bondage" to some *koulak*, or landlord, and fully comprehend how disastrous such a step will be. But a peasant always counts on his luck. He thinks he can scrape up a little money and thus escape usurers altogether. And even when compelled to appeal to their ruinous assistance, the peasant lulls his fears to rest with the hope that some pitying fate will at the last moment befriend him. In any case, times moves slowly, and ruin is as yet far off.

From the taxes there is no escape, and the reckoning day comes quickly. The administration is very exacting as to arrears, for punctuality in collecting taxes constitutes the tax-gatherer's best claim for promotion and the approval of his superiors. No excuse is admitted. Even in times of famine payment of arrears is enforced by the *stanovois* and *ispravniks*. When there is neither corn nor cattle to seize in insolvent villages the police sell houses and storehouses, ploughs and harrows, by auction.

But such drastic measures as these can be resorted to but once in each village; the dispossessed peasants are turned into beggars, and can thenceforth pay nothing more. Administrators who are wise prefer other means, which, while of considerable efficacy, have no disastrous economical consequences, and may, therefore, be repeated every year and to any extent. This is flogging. Insolvent peasants are flogged in a body, in crowds and alone. To show how extensively this forcible administrative method is used in modern Russia, I may mention that during the winter of 1885-6, a tax-inspector of Novgorod province reported that in one district alone 1,500 peasants were condemned to be flogged for non-payment of taxes. Of these, 550 had then been flogged. The remainder were awaiting their turn, and the charitable inspector interceded with the Ministry to procure them a respite.

It is, indeed, open to doubt whether even on the old slave-owners' estates there was ever so extensive an application of the rod as there now is in modern Russia, twenty-five years after the Emancipation.

It will thus be seen that that old ingredient in Russian life, the rod, still plays a very important part in the lives of the peasants. It is at the bottom of the whole system of spoliation, for the tax-collector's rod and nothing else is driving the peasantry under the wheels of the despoiler's machine, which has for its working or peripheral tools the *koulaks*, *mir*-eaters, and usurious landlords.

In the foregoing pages I have described the central or directing organs of the same machine, with its complicated economical network of banks, railways, paper money, and the rest. I have shown, as the reader may remember, that the mainspring of this colossal mechanism, and the final instrument in the abstraction of corn from the mouths of its producers, is the paper money issued by the Government. Put in febrile motion by the banks, and concentrated in the hands of the corn merchants, this money overflows the country in September, and sweeps away with irresistible power the peasants' provision of food.

Thus both keys to the machine are held by the Government. In both cases its action is subservient to that of the capitalists, but in both it works in their favour, giving them the necessary power over the objects, or, let us say, the victims of their manipulations—the peasants. While lending to the capitalists and the higher-class *koulaks* millions of paper money with one hand, the Government with the other hand flogs the peasants into submission to the rural agents and representatives of these capitalists—the *koulaks*, *mir*-eaters, and usurers of every description.

The terrible machine must and will do its work. With the impoverishment of the masses, the drastic measures for extorting taxes will rather become intensified than subside. Having to sustain itself more or less on a level with its powerful Western neighbours, the Empire can neither diminish its expenditure nor arrest the continual increment of the public debt. On the other hand, the more the *koulaks* and *mir*-eaters succeed in their work of devastation the richer they become, and the more are they able to extend their operations. They never have any difficulty in finding investments for their capital in the villages; they have no need to seek candidates for loans. On the contrary, each winter as the taxes fall due, all these village usurers are besieged with suppliants who, imploring their help, submit to every humiliation which a self-satisfied and brutal upstart can inflict, if haply they may obtain from him a loan at cent. per cent.

There is no chance of the havoc being arrested. Even at the present day one-third of our formerly independent peasants are reduced to the state of homeless, down-trodden beggarly *batraks*, and in thirteen provinces the population is literally being starved out at the rate of seventeen per thousand a year. If no change is brought about, we may affirm that in another fifteen years the rate of this *descensus Averni* will be doubled.

But, the reader may well ask, is there no remedy for these heart-sickening horrors? For unless the Opposition can bring forth some practical and acceptable proposals of reform, some scheme for ameliorating the deep-rooted evils here described, their exposition, though it may deepen the shadows and intensify the sorrows of this vale of tears, can serve no useful purpose. The question, therefore, is whether any of the parties forming the Opposition have brought forward some acceptable plan capable of immediate application for the solution of Russian agrarian—which is equal to saying social—difficulties.

Yes, there is such a solution—a solution which has been pointed out not by one, but by every section of the Opposition, by all the thinking men of the country who have studied the question, and, what is more important still, one which is supported unanimously, the *koulaks* alone dissenting, and which enjoys the good wishes of the whole of our agrarian class. Moreover, the peasants' natural good sense has suggested the very same solution of the problem to which men of science have been led by their studies. The peasants must have the land. From sham owners they must be transformed into real proprietors, able to live by their land, pay their taxes, and put something aside for the unforeseen casualties of agrarian life, and for the gradual improvement of the cultivation of the land according to the best methods of science and the teachings of Western experience.

Is Russia sufficiently rich in land to afford the material possibility for such a reform? The question hardly needs answering. Less than one-third (twenty-seven per cent.) of the land capable of cultivation is held by the peasantry; the remaining two-thirds lie as dead capital in the hands of the government or are wasted by the landlords, who either do not cultivate it at all or convert it into an instrument of most reckless extortion. The *kabala* or "bondage" culture we have just described is the only one which exists or can exist on an extensive scale on the landlords' estates in the Russia of to-day. Now though this may be profitable to private individuals, it is absolutely ruinous to the community at large. It destroys a hundred times more wealth on the side of the peasants than it creates on that of the landlords. Neither are our landlords prospering, as I have shown by statistics in an earlier work ("Russian Storm Cloud," p. 57). If transferred to the peasants, this land, or even only a considerable part of it, would more than suffice to set them on a firm footing at once, without requiring either any particular outlay or any additional technical knowledge.

Every average peasant family can, provided it preserve its implements of labour in good repair and the normal number of cattle, cultivate unaided fifty-four acres of land, and can earn its own living and pay its taxes with ease. The prevailing "three fields" system of culture is undoubtedly the clumsiest of its kind; under it only two-thirds of the arable land are utilised at a time, the remaining third being kept fallow in order to restore its fertility. The average return yielded by crops over the whole of Russia is moreover only 2·9 to one grain sown (excluding the seed). This is almost the *minimum*, below which regular agriculture would hardly be possible. But the "three fields" system of rotation is the cheapest form of cultivation, requiring a *minimum* outlay in implements and the smallest quantity of manure; and in the fertile regions of black soil no manure at all. It is the only system possible at the outset. But our agriculture admits of an almost unlimited improvement. *Were the Russian (European) fields cultivated as are those of Great Britain*, says E. Reilus, *Russia would produce, instead of six hun-*

dred and fifty million hectolitres of corn annually, about five milliards, which would be sufficient to feed a population of five hundred million souls. ("Geographie Universelle," vol. v., p. 859.) Add to this the fact that an enormous residue of land is laying in store for future generations. In European Russia the cultivated land is but twenty-one per cent. of the whole area, while it is sixty-one per cent. in Great Britain and eighty-three per cent. in France.

The wealth of Russia in land is enormous, and amply sufficient to transform it from a country of beggars into a land of plenty. The poverty of its husbandmen, compelled to sit on their "cat's plot," whilst enormous tracts of land lie waste around them, is a monstrous crime against nature as well as against humanity. A simple reorganization of our absurd agrarian system will put an end to this, and enable the peasants to start on the work of economical progress and emulation.

The urgency of this reform, the impossibility of going on without it, and the universal desire for it, are guarantees that, were Russia free to assert her will and manage her own affairs, it would speedily be realized. But it is evident that only a free Russia can and will undertake so radical a reform. The decrepit autocracy has neither the moral strength to risk it nor the material means necessary for its accomplishment. All the Government has done by way of satisfying the despairing cry for more land and of silencing the clamour made about it by the democratic part of the press, was the foundation, in May 1882, of the so-called "peasants' land bank," for facilitating the acquisition by peasants of saleable land. The means placed at the disposal of this bank were, however, so small (only five million roubles a year, while the Government pays to the railway shareholders alone an annual tribute of forty-six millions) that the bank is unable to supply even the yearly increase of population with land; and its statutory arrangements are such that it can advance money only to those who already possess something—the *koulaks* and groups of well-to-do peasants, and not the destitute—thus increasing the segregation and concentration of land into a few hands instead of distributing it more widely. Nothing better, indeed, could be expected from our Government.

But let us suppose, for argument's sake, the Autocrat of Russia, head of the privileged of every class—let us suppose him transformed into a Czar-

Democrat such as some foolish *narodniks* have imagined. I affirm that the most radical agrarian reform initiated by him without the abolition of the present political organization would be quite inadequate to permanently improve the condition of our peasantry.

The mischief already wrought by the present system is too deeply seated to be remedied by mere grants of land. Many of the peasants, no fewer than twenty millions, are unable to cultivate the little land they already possess for lack of cattle and implements—that is, in two words—industrial capital. After the grant of new land they can neither start afresh nor rise to material ease without enjoying for a certain time the benefit of cheap credit. Without this aid they would have to apply once more to the *koulaks*, who would demand their two hundred and three hundred per cent., and thus repeat the same process of enslavement and spoliation, only on a larger scale than before.

The reliance placed by our peasants on their collective strength, educated as they are in the traditions of their *mir*,—together with the remarkable honesty, fairness, and sense of duty displayed by these *mirs* in their dealings when they are really independent—greatly facilitate such operations as those in question. The union of the peasants of one village offers a far greater security than any individual landlord can give, always provided, of course, that the *mir* has real and full control over its affairs. A *mir* is, moreover, a natural and permanent assurance company for all its members in case of unforeseen misfortune, acting thus as preserver of the otherwise unstable economical equilibrium.

Under the present *régime* the *mir* plays this part only in exceptional cases, where the commune is not totally destitute. It is generally composed of a mass of beggars, who cannot afford the assistance they would otherwise give, and of a few *koulaks* and *mir*-eaters, who sell their help at the price I have named. Still less can the modern bureaucratic *mir* be trusted with any money, be the amount great or small.

The modern *mir* is completely subject to the local police and the administration, which allow it the free exercise of its powers of self-government only when there is no inducement for officials to interfere. Whenever any profit is to be made the *stanovoi* and *ispravniks* are always at hand, using every means in their power, from threats and ear-boxing to flogging, to enforce their will. The abuse of authority on the part of inferior police agents and administrators, and their cruel treatment of the helpless peasantry, form one of the most sickening and bloody chapters in the annals of Russian autocracy.

The common and unfailing expedient used by these officers for getting their fingers into the pie is to get one of their minions nominated to the post of "head-man" (*volost*) and manager of the communal finances,—of some *koulak* or *mir*-eater—who will repay their support by giving them a share in the booty.

The embezzlement of peasants' money by administrators of this stamp goes on as impudently here as in the Czar's Government generally. It is certainly practised on a more extensive scale in these cases than in the higher walks of political life, which are necessarily under better control. The illiterate peasants are quite defenceless, and should some educated man try to interfere on their behalf he is sure to get into serious trouble, for sympathy with the peasants is always considered in high circles as identical with subversive ideas. Robbery goes on unchecked, hardly concealed by even the forms of decency.

It not infrequently happens that the money paid for taxes is embezzled, the peasant in this case being compelled to pay a second time. The sums sent by the *zemstvos* for the relief of the hungry are embezzled ; the funds advanced for the purchase of seed corn are seized ; the very corn which is stored in communal granaries as a provision for times of scarcity is stolen. Each year brings heaps of such cases to light. All that can be plundered is plundered.

On what ground, then, can we hope that "cheap credit" institutions would escape ? We know by experience how these so-called " peasants' loans and savings banks " are managed, which for a time were the hobby of the *zemstvos* and of the liberal officials. They received a considerable development, their capital amounting in 1883 to thirteen million roubles—on paper, at least. To show what these banks were I need only quote from the *Novoe Vremya*, the organ of the high-class *koulaks*, which admitted that "in an enormous majority of instances the banks benefited the bulk of the peasants nothing whatever, having become instruments of usury in the hands of rural *koulaks* and swindlers." The managers, communal clerks, *koulaks*, parish beadles, and other rural notabilities "borrowed money from the banks to re-lend at usurious interest to needy peasants." (No. 2532.)

Several revisions, undertaken on some occasions by the Governors-General in entire provinces, as for instance in those of the eight districts of Tchernigoff Province and the whole Penza province (1882), have shown that the money was principally "borrowed" by a few persons when the banks first started, some ten or twelve years ago, and has not yet been refunded. To use plain English, it was simply stolen. For formality's sake, a new book was bought every January, and the old debtors' names re-entered from year to year, as if the amounts standing to their debit had been only just advanced. Exactly the same trick was used by Rykoff, Youkhanzeff, and other high-class robbers who stole millions, a fact which only goes to prove yet once again that *les beaux esprits se rencontrent*.

Enough of this. From these cursory remarks the reader can well realize that the second of the great measures indispensable for extricating the peasants from the grasp of usury—cheap credit— would be a rather risky proceeding under the present political *régime*.

The third indispensable requirement for rendering the acquisition, by the people, of the material means of work, of any avail is the spread of both elementary and professional education among the rural classes. A large and wide diffusion of knowledge among them would increase tenfold the productiveness of labour, and open out an unlimited field for further progress in its social and economical life. But here, once more, we stumble against the autocracy, which cannot tolerate the idea of an educated peasantry, and which does not recoil from the most barefaced obstructions and shameful subterfuges for hindering the diffusion of primary education, impeding the foundation of new schools, and blocking the wheels of the old ones.

To conclude. There is a means for extricating our people from the deadlock to which Russia has been brought ; but it implies as a *conditio sine quâ non* the abolition of the bureaucratic despotism and the transformation of the autocratic Empire into a free constitutional State of the European type. Of all the series of measures which only in their totality would suffice to reduce to order the present economical, social, and political chaos, not one can be adopted by the existing *régime*.

Each implies or necessitates the breaking up of the present system. And every step that makes for the redemption of the masses involves danger to the supremacy of the Czar and his satellites.

Our Government, caring above all things for its own interests and privileges, and putting all else in the background, acts according to the dictates of the grossest selfishness. It did not object to reforms in favour of the peasants so long as the reforms could be effected at the expense of the serf-owning nobility. This was very wise and perspicacious, and for a time won the Emperor Alexander II. great popularity, even among extreme Radicals and Socialists. But from the moment when this was found insufficient, and a demand was made for the cessation of absolute power, the Government made up its mind and took the opposite course.

The whole home policy of the two last reigns since the Emancipation, is nothing but a constant fostering of the interests of the privileged classes at the expense of the masses. Hundreds of millions —milliards—of money exacted from the peasants are spent in "supporting the nobility" or the "landlords," or in subsidizing great manufacturers. For the sake of augmenting the profits of the favoured trades, prohibitive tariffs are levied, wars of conquest are undertaken, and conquered provinces cut off by cordons of custom-houses of the interior. And when, in 1871, the more enlightened and liberal part of the privileged classes—the *zemstvos* of all the thirty-four provinces where the *zemstvos* existed—unanimously condemned the injustice of the present fiscal system and petitioned for the introduction of a progressive income-tax, equitable for all, the Czar Alexander II. pronounced the measure to be too democratic and subversive—too likely to injure and alienate the *koulaks*, the usurers, the sharpers and the swindlers of every sort. In its selfish fear autocracy appeals to the worst instincts and the basest elements of human nature, for selfishness and greed is its best support.

Connivance is secured by dividing the booty, and attempts to improve the condition of the masses are regarded as acts of overt sedition. They are opposed by the combined forces of the censorship of the Press and the police. The people's friends are not even allowed to denounce the horrors which are passing under their eyes. The democratic monthlies, such as the *Annales*, the *Slovo*, and the *Dielo*, are suppressed under the pretext that they are organs of "revolution" —a nonsensical accusation against periodicals that had been published for fifteen or eighteen years in the Czar's capital. Their real offence was that they made the investigation of the condition of our peasantry the chief object of their efforts, and continually held the light of truth and science over this abyss of popular suffering.

Whenever some fact or some rumour brings the agrarian question forcibly before the public, the press invariably receives secret orders, like those of June 12th, 1881, and June 26th, 1882, forbidding, "in order not to excite public opinion," the publication of anything referring to the sensational affair of Count Bobrinsky and Prince Scherbatoff, showing such an amount of cruelty, cheating, and malversation on the part of these gentlemen towards the peasantry as to be exceptional and revolting even for Russia. Or the orders are more sweeping, as on March 17th, 1882 :—"It is absolutely forbidden to publish anything referring to the rumours going on among peasants as to the redistribution of land, as well as articles alleging the necessity or the justice of making any alteration in the agrarian condition of the peasants." Or on September

18th, 1885 :—" Forbidding absolutely the commemoration in any form of the coming (February 19th, 1886) twenty-fifth anniversary of the emancipation of the peasants," lest some allusion to their present evil plight might perchance escape the speakers.

This is our position. It is not the Imperial Government that materially or purposely ruins the peasants, which is equivalent to saying the nation; but the Government, out of regard for its mere selfish interests, purposely and deliberately supports and assists those who are ruining it, whilst, for the same reason, suppressing every influence and force likely to produce a different result. The Government of the two Alexanders is, therefore, fully and entirely responsible for the present sufferings of the Russian masses. This is the chief, the most terrible and overwhelming count in the indictment against our Government.

Great are the wrongs, bitter the abuses and sufferings inflicted by this despotism on the whole of educated Rusia—arbitrary arrests, detentions, exiles without any trial whatever, the trampling down of all sacred human rights, suppression of freedom of speech and of the press, violation of the hearth and prevention of the right to work, whereby the lives of thousands of intelligent, well-intentioned, and innocent men and women are either wasted or made miserable. But what are their sufferings compared with those of the dumb millions of our peasantry? What an ocean of sorrow, tears, despair, and degradation is reflected in these dry figures, which prove that households have by hundreds of thousands been forced to sell by auction all their poor possessions; that millions of peasants who were at one time independent have been turned into *batraks*, driven from their homes, have had their families destroyed, their children sold into bondage, and their daughters given to prostitution; and untold numbers of full-grown, nay even gray-haired, respectable labourers, have been shamefully flogged to extort taxes. Then think on these frightful figures of mortality—sixty-two a year per thousand in thirteen provinces. This means nothing less than half a million a year virtually dying of hunger, starved to death in a twelvemonth, with the probability that before long the proportion will be doubled.

Verily, it is here, and not so much in the cruelties inflicted on political offenders, that we must look for the cause of the fierce, implacable hatred of the revolutionists against their Government.

Herein lies the peremptory cause, the permanent stimulant and the highest justification of the Russian revolution and of Russian conspiracies. Life is not worth living when your eyes constantly behold such miseries as these inflicted on a people whom you love. It would be a shame to bear the name of a Russian had these unutterable sufferings of the masses called forth no responsive and boundless devotion to the people's cause ; a devotion which glows in the hearts of all those thousands of Russia's sons and daughters who risk life, freedom, domestic happiness, all which is most dear to our common nature, in the effort to free their country from a Government which is the mainspring of all these woes.

But, we are sometimes told, the Nihilists have no right to set themselves up as champions of the peasants against the autocracy, for the rural masses are loyal and devoted to the Czar.

If to label aspirations which, in their very essence, are hostile to the Czardom with the name of the Czar can in truth be called loyalty, why then a vast majority of our peasants are most assuredly very loyal indeed. In this case, however, it is strange that the Imperial Government and the Czar himself place so little trust in this loyalty as to tremble at the thought of putting it to the test. The prospect of perpetual Nihilist attempts, which make the present life of the Gatschina prisoner a burden and the future a terror, seem to the Government preferable to the chances of a popular vote. For have not the Nihilists repeatedly declared that they would desist from hostilities towards their paternal government from the first moment that it obtained the sanction of the freely expressed voice of the people?

The fact is that the peasants are as dissatisfied with the working of the present institutions as the Nihilists themselves—certainly more dissatisfied than are the educated and privileged classes as a whole. And the reader will certainly admit that for this discontent they have ample cause. The only difference between the middle-class opposition and the peasantry is, that the peasantry think the autocracy has no share whatever in bringing on them the calamities from which they suffer, and that the Czar is as much dissatisfied as the peasants themselves with the present order of things, which they attribute to the wickedness and cunning of the "nobility." It is doubtful whether the peasants will stick for ever, or for long, to this nonsensical idea. But I frankly confess that, even as matters now stand, I take a totally different view as to this would-be sanction. I think that if there be anything which deprives our Government of all claim to respect; if there be anything which can lower it in the eyes of mankind, and which will remain as a stain on its escutcheon for evermore, it is just the foul perfidy involved in the abuse of this touching, child-like confidence reposed in it by the simple-hearted millions of our Russian peasantry.

THE MOUJIKS AND THE RUSSIAN DEMOCRACY.

CHAPTER I.

WHEN, about a score of years before the Emancipation, the Russian democrats for the first time came into close contact with the peasants, with the view of becoming better acquainted with their down-trodden brothers, they were amazed at their discoveries. The *moujiks* proved to be an entirely different race from what pitying people amongst their "elder brothers" expected them to be.

Far from being degraded and brutalised by slavery, the peasants, united in their semi-patriarchal, semi-republican village communes, exhibited a great share of self-respect, and even capacity to stand boldly by their rights, where the whole of the commune was concerned. Diffident in their dealings with strangers, they showed a remarkable truthfulness and frankness in their dealings among themselves, and a sense of duty and loyalty and unselfish devotion to their little communes, which contrasted strikingly with the shameful corruption. and depravity of the official classes.

They had not the slightest notion of the progress made by the sciences, and believed that the earth rested on three whales, swimming on the Ocean; but in their traditional morality they sometimes showed such deep humanity and wisdom as to strike their educated observers with wonder and admiration.

These pioneer democrats, men of great talent and enormous erudition, such as Yakushkin, Dal, and Kireevsky, in propagating among the bulk of the reading public the results of their long years of study, laid the base of that democratic feeling which has never since died out in Russia.

From that time forth the momentous rush of the educated people "amongst the peasants," and the study of the various sides of peasant life, has been constantly on the increase. No country possesses such a literature on the subject as Russia; but the tone of the writers of these latter times—men of the same stamp as Yakushkin and Kireevsky—is no longer that of unmixed admiration. Whether you embark on the sea of statistical and ethnographical lore collected for posterity by the untiring zeal of the late Orloff and his followers, or whether you are lost in admiration of the artistic sketches of peasant life drawn by Uspensky, or whether you are perusing the works of no less trustworthy though less gifted essayists of the same school, such as Zlatovratsky and Zassodimsky, you will invariably be brought to recognise a great breaking up of the traditional groundwork of the social and moral life of our peasantry.

Something harsh, cruel, cynically egotistical, is worming itself into the hearts of the Russian agricultural population, where formerly all was simplicity, peace, and goodwill unto men. Thus the grey-bearded grandfathers are not alone in modern Russia in lamenting the good old times. Some of our young and popular writers are, strangely enough, striking the same wailing chords. It is evident that in the terrible straits through which our people are passing, not only their material condition but their very souls have suffered grave injuries.

Yet it is not all lamentation about the past in the tidings which reach us from our villages. The good produced by the progress of culture is, in spite of its drawbacks, according to our modest opinion, full compensation for the impairing of the almost unconscious virtues of the old patriarchal period.

Freed from the yoke of serfdom, and put before the tribunals on an equal footing with other citizens, their former masters included, the peasants, too, are beginning to feel themselves to be citizens. A new generation, which has not known slavery, has had time to grow up. Their aspiration after independence has not as yet directed itself against political despotism, save in isolated cases; but in the meantime it has almost triumphed in the struggle against the more intimate and trying domestic despotism of the *bolshak*, the head of the household. A very important and thoroughgoing change has taken place in the family relations of the great Russian rural population. The children, as soon as they are grown up and have married, will no longer submit to the *bolshak's* whimsical rule. They rebel, and if imposed upon, separate and found new households, where they become masters of their own actions. These separations have grown so frequent that the number of independent households in the period from 1858-1881 increased from thirty-two per cent. to seventy-one per cent. of the whole provincial population.

It is worthy of remark that the rebellion among the educated classes also first began in the circle of domestic life, before stepping into the larger arena of political action.

Elementary education, however hampered and obstructed by the Government, is spreading among the rural classes. In 1868, of a hundred recruits of peasant origin there were only eight who could read and write. In 1882 the proportion of literate people among the same number was twenty. This is little compared with what might have been done, but it is a great success if we remember the hindrances the peasant has had to overcome.

Reading, which a score of years ago was confined exclusively to the upper classes, is now spreading among the *moujiks*. Popular literature of all kinds has received an unprecedented development in the last ten or fifteen years. Popular books run through dozens of editions, and are selling by scores of thousands of copies.

Religion is the language in which the human spirit lisps its first conceptions of right and gives vent to its first aspirations. The awakening of the popular intelligence and moral consciousness has found its expression in dozens of new religious sects, a remarkable and suggestive phenomenon of modern popular life in Russia. Differing entirely from the old ritualistic sectarianism, which was more of a rebellion against ecclesiastical arrangements than against orthodoxy, these new sects of rationalistic and Protestant type have acquired in about ten or twelve years hundreds of thousands, nay millions, of proselytes.

This movement of thought, both by its exaltation and the general tendency of its doctrines, can be compared with the great Protestant movement of the sixteenth century. The only difference consists in its being confined in Russia exclusively to the rural and working classes, without being in the least shared by the educated people. The sources of religious enthusiasm are dried up, we think for ever, in the Russian intellectual classes, their enthusiasm and exaltation having found quite another vent. For nobody can seriously consider the few drawing-room attempts to found some new creed, of which we have now and then heard of late. But it is beyond doubt that the genuine and earnest development of religious thoughts and feelings, which we are witnessing among our masses, will play an important part in our people's near future.

In whatever direction we look, everything proves that under the apparent calm there is a great movement in the minds of our rural population. The great social and political crisis, through which Russia is passing, is not confined to the upper classes alone. The process of demolition, slower but vaster, is going on among the masses too. There all is tottering to its fall—orthodoxy, custom, traditional forms of life. The European public only takes notice of the upper stratum of the crisis, of that which is going on among the educated, because of its dramatic manifestations ; but the crisis among our agricultural classes, wrought by the combined efforts of civilisation on the one hand and of economical ruin on the other, is no less real, and certainly no less interesting and worthy of study than the former.

In what does this crisis consist? How far and in what direction have the changes in the social and ethical ideals, the traditional morality and the character of the *moujik*, the tiller and guardian of our native land, gone? It would seem presumption to answer, or even to attempt to answer, in the space of a few pages such questions in reference to an enormous rural population like the Russian. I hasten, therefore, to mention one thing which renders such an attempt—partial at least—justifiable.

A Russian *moujik* presents of course as many varieties as there are tribes and regions in the vast empire. There is a wide difference between the peculiarly sociable, open-hearted Great Russian peasant, brisk in mind and speech, quick to love and quick to forget, and the dreamy and reserved Ruthenian; or between the practical, extremely versatile and independent Siberian, who never knew slavery, and the timid Beloruss (White Russian), who has borne three yokes. But through all the varieties of types, tribes, and past history, the millions of our rural population present a remarkable uniformity in those higher general, ethical, and social conceptions which the educated draw from divers social and political sciences, and the uneducated from their traditions, which are the depositories of the collective wisdom of past generations.

This seemingly strange uniformity in our peasants' moral physiognomy is to be accounted for by two causes: the perfect identity of our people's daily occupation, which is almost exclusively pure husbandry, and the great similitude of those peculiar self-governing associations, village communes, in which the whole of our rural population, without distinction of tribe or place, have lived from time immemorial.

No occupation is fitter to develop a morally as well as physically healthy race than husbandry. We mean genuine husbandry, where the tiller of the soil is at the same time its owner. We need not dwell on the proofs. Poets, historians, and philosophers alike have done their best to bring home to us, corrupted children of the towns, the charms of the simple virtues which hold sway amidst the populations of staunch ploughmen.

In Russia, until the "economic progress" of the last twenty-five years turned twenty millions of our peasants into landless proletarians, they were all landowners. Even the scourge of serfdom could not depose them from that dignity. The serfs, who gratuitously tilled the manorial land, had each of them pieces of freehold land which they cultivated on their own account. Nominally it was the property of the landlords. But so strong was tradition and custom that the landlords themselves had almost forgotten that they had a right to it. So much was this the case that Professor Engelhardt ("Letters from a Village"), tells us that many of the former seigneurs only learned from the Act of Emancipation of 1861 that the land on which the peasants dwelt also belonged to them.

Gleb Uspensky, in discussing the causes of the wonderful preservation of the purity of the moral character of the Russian people through such a terrible ordeal as three centuries of slavery, which passed over without ingrafting into it any of the vice of slavery, can find no other explanation than this: the peasant was never separated from the ploughshare, from the all-absorbing cares and the poetry of agricultural work.

Our peasants could, however, do something more than preserve their individuality. They could give a môre lasting proof and testimony as to their collective dispositions and aspirations. A Russian village has never been a mere aggregation of individuals, but a very intimate association, having much work and life in common. These associations are called *mirs* among the Great and White Russians, *hromadas* among the Ruthenians.

Up to the present time the law has allowed them a considerable amount of self-government. They are free to manage all their economical concerns in common: the land, if they hold it as common property—which is the case everywhere save in the Ruthenian provinces—the forests, the fisheries, the renting of public-houses standing on their territory, etc. They distribute among themselves as they choose, the taxes falling to the share of the commune according to the Government schedules. They elect the rural executive administration—*Starost* and *Starshinas*—who are (nominally at least) under their permanent control.

Another very important privilege which they possess is that they, the village communes composing the *Volost*, in general meeting assembled, elect the ten judges of the *Volost*. All these must be peasants, members of some village commune. The jurisdiction of the peasants' tribunal is very extensive; all the civil, and a good many criminal offences (save the capital ones), in which one of the parties, at least, is a peasant of the district, are amenable to it. The peasants sitting as judges are not bound to abide in their verdicts by the official code of law. They administer justice according to the customary laws and traditions of the local peasantry.

The records of these tribunals, published by an official commission, at once afford us an insight into the peasants' original notions as to juridical questions. We pass over the verdicts illustrating the popular idea as to land tenure, which has been expounded above. We will rather try to elicit the other side of the question : the peasants' views on movable property, the right of bequest, of inheritance, and their civil code in general, which presents some curious and unexpected peculiarities.

The fact which strikes us most in it is, that among the peasants where the patriarchal principle is as yet so strong and the ties of blood are held so sacred, kinship gives no right to property. The only rightful claim to it is given by work. Whenever the two interests clash, it is to the right of labour that the popular conscience gives the preference. The father cannot disinherit one son or diminish his share for the benefit of his favourite. Notwithstanding the religious respect in which the last will of a dying man is held, both the *mir* and the tribunal will annul it at the complaint of the wronged man, if the latter is known to be a good and diligent worker. The fathers themselves know this well. Whenever they attempt to prejudice one of their children in their wills they always adduce as motive that he has been a sluggard or a spendthrift and has already dissipated his share. The favourite, on the other hand, is mentioned as "having worked hard for the family."

Kinship has no influence whatever in the distribution and proportioning of shares at any division of property. It is determined by the quantity of work each has given to the family. The brother who has lived and worked with the family for the longer time will receive most, no matter whether he be the elder or the younger. He will be excluded from the inheritance altogether if he has been living somewhere else and has not contributed in some way to the common expenses. The same principle is observed in settling the differences between the other grades of kinsfolk. The cases of sons in-law, step-sons, and adopted children are very characteristic. If they have remained a sufficient time—ten or more years—with the family, they receive, though strangers, all the rights of legitimate children, whilst the legitimate son is excluded if he have not taken part in the common work.

This is in flagrant contradiction to the civil code of Russia, as well as of other European countries. The same contradiction is observable in the question of women's rights. The Russian law entitles women—legitimate wives and daughters—to *one-fourteenth* only of the family inheritance. The peasants' customary law requires no such limitation. The women are in all respects dealt with on an equal footing with the men. They share in the property in proportion to their share in the work. Sisters, as a rule, do not inherit from brothers, because in marrying they go to another family, and take with them as dowry the reward of their domestic work. But a spinster sister, or a widow who returns to live with her brothers, will always receive or obtain from the tribunal her share.

The right to inheritance being founded on work alone, no distinction is made by the peasants' customary law between legitimate wives and concubines.

It is interesting to note that the husband, too, inherits the wife's property (if she has brought him any) only when they have lived together sufficiently long—above ten years; otherwise the deceased wife's property is returned to her parents.

The principle ruling the order of inheritance is evidently the basis for the verdicts in all sorts of litigation. Labour is always recognized as giving an indefeasible right to property. According to common jurisprudence, if one man has sown a field belonging to another—especially if he has done it knowingly—the court of justice will unhesitatingly deny the offender any right to the eventual product. Our peasants are as strict in their observance of boundaries, when once traced, as are any other agricultural folk. But labour has its imprescriptible rights. The customary law prescribes a remuneration for the work executed *in both* of the above mentioned cases—in the case of unintentional as well as in the case of premeditated violation of property. Only, in the first instance, the offender, who retains all the product, is simply compelled to pay to the owner the rent of the piece of land he has sown, according to current prices, with some trifling additional present ; whilst in the case of violation knowingly done, the product is left to the owner of the land, who is bound, nevertheless, to return to the offender the seed, and to pay him a labourer's wages for the work he has done.

If a peasant has cut wood in a forest belonging to another peasant, the tribunal settles the matter in a similar way. In all these cases the common law would have been wholly against the offender, the abstract right of property reigning supreme.

In the vast practice of the many thousands of peasants' tribunals, there are certainly instances of verdicts being given on other principles than these, or contrary to any principle whatever. Remembering the very numerous influences to which a modern village is subjected in these critical times, it would have been surprising were it otherwise. Moreover, the peasants' tribunal has by its side the *pissar*, the communal clerk, a stranger to the village and its customs. This important person is the champion and propagator of official views and of the official code. His influence on the decisions of the peasants' courts is considerable, as is well known. The rarity of the exceptions, however, makes the rule the more salient.

The peasants have applied their collective intelligence not to material questions alone, nor within the domain apportioned to them by law. The *mir* recognises no restraint on its autonomy. In the opinion of the peasants themselves, the *mir's* authority embraces, indeed, all domains and branches of peasant life. Unless the police and the local officers are at hand to prevent what is considered an abuse of power, the peasants' *mir* is always likely to exceed its authority.

Here is a curious illustration. In the autumn of 1884, according to the *Russian Courier* of the 12th November, 1884, a peasants' *mir* in the district of Radomysl had to pronounce upon the following delicate petition : One of their fellow-villagers, Theodor P., whose wife had run away from him several years before, and who was living as housemaid in some private house, wanted to marry another woman from a neighbouring village. He accordingly asked the *mir* to accept his bride as a female member of their commune. Having heard and discussed this original demand, the *mir* unanimously passed the following resolution : " Taking into consideration that the peasant Theodor P., living for several years without his legitimate wife by the fault of the latter, is now in great need of a woman (!), his marriage with the former wife is dissolved. In accordance with which, after being thrice questioned by the elder (mayor) of our village as to whether we will permit Theodor P. to receive into his house as wife the peasant woman N——, we give our full consent thereto. And if, moreover, Theodor P. shall have children by his second wife, we will recognise them as legitimate and as heirs to their father's property, the freehold and the communal land included."

This resolution, duly put on paper and signed by all the householders and by the elder of the village, was delivered as certificate of marriage to the happy couple, no one suspecting that the *mir* had overstepped its power.

In the olden times, as late as the sixteenth century, it was the *mir* who elected the parson (as the dissenting villages are doing nowadays), the bishops only imposing hands on the *mir's* nominees. The orthodox peasants have quite forgotten this historical right of theirs; but the natural right of the *mir* allows it to deal even with subjects referring to religion.

The conversion to dissenting creeds of whole villages in a lump, is of very common occurrence in the history of modern sects. A dissenting preacher comes to a village and makes a few converts. For a time they zealously preach their doctrines to their fellow-villagers. Then, when they consider the harvest ripe, they bring the matter before the *mir*, and often that assembly, after discussing the question, passes a resolution in favour of the acceptance of the new creed. The whole village turns "shaloput" or "evangelical," changing creeds as small states did in the times of the Reformation.

To a Russian peasant it seems the most natural thing in the world that the *mir* should do this whenever it chooses. In my wanderings among the peasants, I remember having met near Riazan with a peasant who amused me much by telling how they succeeded in putting a check on the cupidity and extortion of the *pop* of their village. "When we could no longer bear it we assembled and said to him, 'Take care, batka (father); if you won't be reasonable, we, all the *mir*, will give up orthodoxy altogether, and will elect a *pop* from among ourselves.'" And the *pop* then became "tender as silk," for he knew his flock would not hesitate to put their threat into effect.

The *mir* forms indeed a *microcosm*, a small world of its own. The people living in it have to exercise their judgment on everything, on the moral side of man's life as on the material, shaping it so as to afford to their small communities as much peace and happiness as is possible under their very arduous circumstances.

Have these uneducated people been able to achieve anything in the high domain of public morality?

Yes, they have, though what they have done cannot be registered in volumes like the verdicts of their tribunals. They have maintained througn centuries, and improved, the old Russian principle of governing without oppression. To settle all public questions by unanimous vote, never by mere majority, is a wise rule, for a body of people living on such close terms. This system, however, could only be rendered practicable, amongst people of all sorts of tempers and diverse moral qualities, by a high development of the sentiments of justice, equanimity, and conciliation.

Our peasants lay no claim to being a race of Arcadian pastors. Their present and their past alike has been and still is too hard to make it possible for them ever to forget that charity begins at home. In the bitter struggle for a bare existence which they have had to sustain, each has had to consider his own skin first. In their every day life and intercourse they are as egotistical as any other set of people, each man trying to make the best of his opportunities.

"Each for himself," say they—"but God and the *mir* for all." The *mir* is no egotist; it pities everybody alike, and should it have to settle any difference it does not look to the numerical strength or respective influence of the contending parties, but to the absolute justice of the cause.

But is not the *mir* composed of the selfsame individuals who outside of its charmed circle are pursuing each his personal ends and interests? If they are able to forget themselves when at the *mir*, and can elevate their minds and hearts to the exercise of perfect justice and impartiality, they must also be equal to doing the same outside of the *mir*, in those solemn moments when daily cares and anxieties are cast on one side and their higher nature has free play. The *mir's* morality gives its tone to, and shapes according to its image, the morality of the individual too.

Hence that wide tolerance which characterises our peasants; that somewhat gregarious benevolence embracing all men, almost to the prejudice of intensity of personal attachment, but which excludes nobody from its pale. The Russian *moujik* is proverbially benevolent towards strangers of his own race. He is accustomed to feel something like family attachment to most, or to very many, of the members of his *mir*. It is easy for him to admit a new member into so large a family. When difference of religion and of language do not allow of the full benefit of adoption—he will still recognise in the stranger a man like himself.

There is no people on the face of the earth who treat aliens so kindly as do the Russian *moujiks*. They live peacefully side by side with hundreds of tribes, differing in race and religion —Tartars, Circassians, Bouriats, and German colonists. (The outburst against the Jews sprang from economical causes, and not from racial antipathy.) During the last Turkish war, whilst the burghers and the shop-boys of the towns were casting stones and mud at the poor Turkish prisoners of war, as they passed along the streets, until the police had to intervene, the *moujiks* offered them bread and coppers, and in some cases even took them home to their villages as paid labourers. They were greatly perplexed, it is true, as to whether they could invite them to share their meals, being "infidels," but they generally ended by conquering their prejudices;

and they, the representatives of two belligerent nations, might be seen amicably eating at the same table (Zlatovratsey).

The *mir* in the management of its affairs recognises no permanent laws restricting or guiding its decisions. It is the personification of the living law, speaking through the collective voice of the commune. Every case brought before the *mir* is judged on its own merits, according to the endless variety of its peculiar circumstances. In foreign lands, too, the laws tacitly acknowledge the necessity for making a considerable allowance for the voice of pure conscience in the more delicate questions of society—as to the culpability or innocence of its members. But by the side of the jury sits the judge, the representative of the written law, one of whose duties it is to control and keep them within their strictly defined limits—*i.e.*, to the mere verdict as to the facts of the case. With a Russian *mir* the law is nowhere, the "conscience" everywhere. Not merely the fact of the criminal offence, but every disputed point is settled according to the individual justice of the case, no regard being paid to the category of crime to which it may chance to belong.

These villagers have to deal with living men whom they know and love, and it is deeply repugnant to them to overshoot the mark by so much as a hair's breadth for the sake of a dead abstraction—the law.

This bent of mind is not confined to the peasantry,—it is national.

I have frequently observed, and I believe that all who have given any attention to the subject will agree with me, that the abstract idea of "law," as a something which is to be obeyed to the letter under all circumstances, even when the peculiar circumstances of a case make it unjust, is grasped with the greatest difficulty, even by the most cultured Russians.

There are few among our countrymen who will not give the preference to the dictates of conscience tempered by a fair and impartial mind. They are in this respect a perfect contrast to the people of English origin. In our great poet Pushkin this feeling was so strong as to make him an upholder of the principle of absolute monarchy. "Why," he said, "is it necessary that one of us should be put above all the rest, and even above the laws? Because the law is a wooden thing. In the law the man feels something hard, unbrotherly. With a literal application of the law you cannot do much. But at the same time nobody may take upon himself to transgress or disregard the law. Hence it is necessary that there should be a supreme clemency to temper the laws, and this can only be embodied in the autocratic monarch."

Out of respect to the memory of our great national teacher of art, I will not here discuss the antiquated conception of a monarch as a dispenser of justice, and not as an administrator, bound to know all, to see all, to understand all, under penalty of being befooled and made a tool of at every turn. I simply mention it as a good illustration of the peculiar bent of the Russian mind.

Much of this is to be ascribed to the lack of political education, and to the feeble development of the proud and powerful sense of individuality which is the one quality we most envy our Western neighbours. To a truly independent man even a hard law, because abstract and dispassionate, and known to him beforehand, is a better thing than the most benignant despotism. That which is the most abhorrent to him is the sense that he is dependent on the good pleasure of another—be it the benevolent despotism of one master or even the still more benevolent despotism of a friendly crowd.

Nevertheless we must not forget that on the other hand we have been spared the habit of not looking or caring to look beyond the mere legal aspect and established rule as to human conduct.

In constantly striving after individual justice, both in practice, as with the peasants, and in theory, as with the educated classes, our people have not been able to rest satisfied with mere appearances, nor to consider the question solved as soon as they discovered under which section of the criminal or any other code the trespass fell. They have had to look into the very innermost recesses of the human heart, to discover all its hidden promptings, and to subject them to an impartial, dispassionate examination, all which must needs have educated our people in a spirit of the highest tolerance. "To understand everything is to forgive everything," is the deepest of human sayings.

Hence that "pity for all" which extends, not merely to the weak, but to the fallen, to the degraded, to the outcast. Just observe how our *moujiks* behave towards criminals. All, without distinction, are designated under the generic term of "unhappy," and are treated as such. No contempt, no harshness can be detected in the demeanour of the crowd of peasants, who meet (bearing alms in their hands) a body of convicts being escorted to Siberia. They know that many of them must be innocent of any real offence. But there is something deeper than this in their humanity. Gogol, who excelled all other writers in the insight he possessed as to the workings of the Russian mind, observes that "of all nations the Russian alone is convinced that there exists no man who is absolutely guilty, as there exists no man who is absolutely innocent." Is it not this same idea which permeates Dostoievsky's masterpiece, "Buried Alive"? Is not this "pity for all" apparent throughout the works of all our great masters, from Gogol to Gonciaroff and Ostrovsky? Herein lies yet one more proof that in the moral qualities of the two extreme sections of the Russian nation—the peasantry, who are at the bottom of the social scale, and the educated, who are at the top—there are some striking resemblances which cannot be purely accidental.

Many foreign writers have been struck by the peculiar ardour which animates the Russians of all classes in their devotion to their country.

Well, I do not know whether this is due to the emotional character of our people, or whether it is merely a reflection of what is intensely developed under another name within our masses. Among the peasantry, in whose eyes their *mir* is their country, the devotion of each individual to the *mir* has been made the keynote of social morality. They have learned to exercise self-restraint in petty everyday concessions and services to the *mir*, and have risen to the sublimity of heroism in their acts of self-sacrifice for its good. Examples of this are frequent. To "suffer for the *mir;*" to be put in chains and to be thrown into prison as the *mir's khodok* or messenger,—"sent to the Czar" with the *mir's* grievances; to be beaten, exiled to Siberia or to the mines, for having stood up boldly for the rights of the *mir* against some powerful oppressor,—such are the forms of heroism to which an enthusiastic peasant aspires, and which the people extol.

The orthodox Church has no hold over the souls of the masses. The *pop* or priest is but an official of the bureaucracy and depredator of the commune. But we hardly need to say that the high ethics of Christianity, the appeal to brotherly love, to forgiveness, to self-sacrifice for the good of others, yet have always found an echo in the responsive chords of our people's hearts. " The type of a saint, as conceived by our peasants," says Uspensky, "is not that of an anchorite, timidly secluded from the world, lest some part of the treasure he is accumulating in heaven might get damaged. Our popular saint is a man of the *mir*, a man of practical piety, a teacher and benefactor of the people." In Athanasieff's collection of popular legends we find an illustration of this idea. Two saints—St. Cassian and St. Nicolas—have come before the face of the Lord.

"What hast thou seen on the earth?" asks the Lord of St. Cassian, who first approached. " I have seen a *moujik* foundering with his car in a marsh by the wayside."

"Why hast thou not helped him?" " Because I was coming into Thy presence, and was afraid of spoiling my bright clothes."

The turn of St. Nicolas comes, who approaches with his dress all besmeared.

"Why comest thou so dirty into my presence?' asks the Lord. "Because I was following St. Cassian, and, seeing the *moujik* of whom he just spoke, I have helped him out of the marsh."

"Well," said the Lord, "because thou, Cassian, hast cared so much about thy dress and so little about thy brother, I will give thee thy saint's day only once in four years. And to thee, Nicolas, for having acted as thou didst, I will give four saint's days each year."

That is why St. Cassian's Day falls on the 29th of February, in leap year, and St. Nicolas has a saint's day each quarter.

Such is the peasant's interpretation of Christian morality. And is it not suggestive that the greatest novelist of our time, and a man of such vast intelligence as Count Leo Tolstoi, in making his attempt to found a purely ethical religion, formulates his views by referring the educated classes to the gospel *as it is understood by the moujik* ?

Since I do not in the least presume to sketch anything like a full picture of our people's moral physiognomy, I shall stop here. My sole object has been to show that our peasantry, on the whole, as it has entered into political life and freedom after centuries of internal growth, presents a race with highly developed social instincts and many elements promising further progress ; and that the feelings of deep respect, sometimes of enthusiastic admiration, which the Russian democrats feel for the peasantry, are not devoid of foundation.

These feelings may often have been exaggerated, especially of old, when the two classes for the first time came into close contact. But excess of idealisation and sentimentality have become matters of history. They were destroyed by the rough touch of reality; and the mighty figure of the hero of the plough has lost nothing by being stripped of tinsel. Hewn in unpolished stone, he looks better than when robed in marble. The charm of his strength, dauntless courage, and his moral character is strengthened by the thrilling voice of pity for the overwhelming, the indescribable sufferings of this childlike giant. A passion for Equality and Fraternity is and will ever be the strongest, we may say the only strong social feeling in Russia. It is by no means the privilege of "Nihilists," or advanced parties of any kind; it is shared by the enormous majority of our educated classes.

Man is a sociable being. He yearns to attach himself to something vaster than a family, having a longer existence than his immediate surroundings. The feeling in which this yearning finds its commonest and easiest expression is patriotism, embracing the whole of the nation, the State and the people being blended into one. For us Russians, no such blending is possible. The crimes, the cruelties, equalled only by the folly, of those who are representing Russia as a State, stand there to prevent it.

No, no true Russian can ever wish Godspeed to the Government of his country. And yet we Russians are most ardent patriots. We have no attachment to our birthplace or any particular locality. But we love our people, our race, as intensely and organically as the Jews. And we are almost as incapable of getting thoroughly acclimatised in any other nation. In describing Russia's real and not fictitious glories, in speaking when in an expansive mood about his country's probable future and the service she is likely to render to mankind, a Russian can startle a *Chauviniste* of the *grande nation*. Yes, we are certainly patriotic. Only our patriotism runs entirely towards the realisation of the democratic ideal. The idea of country is embodied for us not in our State but in our people, in the *moujiks* and in those various elements which make the *moujiks'* cause our own. Our hopes, our devotion, our love, and that irresistible idealism which stimulates to great labour, all that constitutes the essence of patriotism, with us is democratic.

In the following chapters I will relate how our popular notions of morality and justice bore the test of adversity; what was the form assumed in villages by the corrosive elements, and how the people defended their traditional ideals of life.

We will begin by briefly sketching the tendencies of the purely political elements newly introduced into Russian village life, as they are more circumscribed in their action and far less widespread than the economical.

PATERNAL GOVERNMENT

CHAPTER I.

As soon as the government had earnestly set its mind on the emancipation of the serfs, the all-important questions had to be faced, as to how all these millions of newly-made citizens should be managed and kept in order; and how they should be made to pay the price of their redemption to the lords of the manors, and the taxes to the State? The bureaucratic commission appointed for the settlement of this great problem of the Emancipation, with usual bureaucratic foresight and profundity, at first proposed that to the former *seigneurs* should be entrusted the administration, the justice, and the police of the rural districts.

This would have been neither more nor less than a re-instatement, only in another form, of serfdom—a joke made all the more dangerous in that there was but too much reason to anticipate bitter disappointments on the part of the people on many other points connected with their liberation. Fortunately for itself, the Government listened to wiser counsel, offered by local committees, and the press, which pointed to the village communes as to natural and long-established institutions standing ready to their hand and existing throughout the country. The village commune was preserved. The open-air meetings of all the peasants, the *mir*, were acknowledged as the chief authority both in the village commune and in the rural *volost* or district, an administrative unit embracing a few village communes.

But here most puzzling questions of detail presented themselves to the minds of the St. Petersburg legislators. Notwithstanding the benevolent regard for the peasants which prevailed at this epoch in the highest governmental circles, our lawgivers could not admit that the *mir* might be left just as they found it. It was more than the most refined bureaucratic mind could digest—the *mir* and the *tchin!* It was as though two cultures, two different worlds, we may almost say two different types of human nature, as strongly individualized as they were antipathetic, had suddenly been brought face to face.

What is a *tchinovnik?* It is a man convinced that were it not for his "prescriptions," "instruc-

tions," and "enjoinments" the world would go
all askew, and the people would suddenly begin
to drink ink instead of water, to put their breeches
on their heads instead of on their legs, and to
commit all sorts of other incongruities. As all
his life is passed from his most tender youth
upward in offices, amidst heaps of scribbled papers,
in complete isolation from any touch with real
life, the *tchinovnik* understands nothing, has
faith in nothing but these papers. He is as
desperately sceptical as regards human nature as
a monk, and does not trust one atom to men's
virtue, honesty, or truthfulness. There is nothing
in the world which can be relied upon but
scribbled papers, and he is their votary.

Such an institution as the *mir*—a self-governing
body with no trace of hierarchy or distinction of
ranks, wielding an authority so extensive that in
its own sphere of action it might be called unlimited, and at the same time wishing for no
record of its proceedings, confiding in people's
good faith and the infallible guidance of such a
thing as collective conscience and wisdom—such
an institution as the *mir*, to the mind of a
tchinovnik, must have appeared incoherent, incomprehensible, almost contrary to the laws of

nature. It was his most sacred duty to bring order into this chaos.

Every Russian village commune elects its elder or mayor, who is by virtue of his office its spokesman and delegate before the authorities. In the village itself the elder is neither the chief nor even the *primus inter pares*, but simply the trusted servant and executor of the orders of the *mir*. The *mir* discusses and regulates everything that falls within its narrow and simple sphere of action, leaving hardly anything to the discrimination and judgment of its agent. So simple and subordinate are the elder's duties, that any peasant, provided he be neither a drunkard nor a thief, is eligible for the post. In many villages, in order to avoid discussion, the office of elder is filled in turn by all the members of the *mir*. As the eldership brings the peasant into frequent, almost daily, contact with the administration, which involves him in endless trouble and annoyance, peasants show very little ambition to fill the office. Much persuasion, sometimes remonstrance and abuse, are necessary before an honest peasant, who has not the feathering of his nest in view at the expense of the commune, can be induced to accept this post of honour.

Some writers—Mr. Mackenzie Wallace among them—in describing Russian village life, wonder at this strange lack of political ambition. I think it only too natural: our *moujiks* have not studied the history of Rome, Athens, and other republics, nor do they so much as suspect the existence of great municipalities such as London, Paris, or New York. No obsequious imagination suggests to them flattering analogies, and they cannot see that the proffered dignity is anything but a double servitude—to the *mir* on the one hand and to the administration on the other with no room whatever for the proud self-assertion which gives the charm of office to the gifted; a burden and a public work, differing from those of mending the roads, digging wells, or transporting Government freights only in so far that it is more trying and more troublesome.

Now, in modifying the system of rural self-government the St. Petersburg *tchinovniks* were inspired to transform this very modest and humble village elder into a diminutive *tchinovnik*, created in their own image and likeness. The task was not without its difficulties. The elder was as a rule deficient in the most essential qualification for his profession—he could not write! It was therefore necessary that he should be provided with a secretary, who could inscribe the paper to which he should affix his seal or his cross. This important person, the clerk, was generally a perfect stranger to the village, a man picked up from the streets. As the law must needs give him extensive powers, it was all the more desirable that he should be easily controlled.

Our legislators proved equal to their task; for they blessed our villagers with a system of law-court proceedings which would do honour to much bigger places. To give some idea of their method, suffice it to say that the clerk of the *volost* is bound to supply his office with no less than sixty-five different registers, wherein to keep a record of the sixty-five various papers he has to issue daily, monthly, or quarterly. This was pushing their solicitude for the welfare of the countrymen rather too far, and taxing the clerk's powers rather too highly. In some of the larger *volosts* one man does not suffice for the task, and the peasants are compelled to maintain two, nay, even three clerks. It is needless to add that such a complication of legal business can in no way keep an adroit clerk in check nor prevent the abuse of his power. The opposite is rather the case. The figure cut by the *pissar* or clerk in the annals of our new rural local government is a most unseemly one indeed. In its earlier period it was decidedly its blackest point.

The Government has undoubtedly had a hand in making the *pissar* such a disreputable character, by expressly prohibiting the engagement for this office of men of good education,—for fear of a revolution. All who have completed their studies at a gymnasium (college), much more those who have attended a high school, are precluded from filling this post. Only the more ignorant, those who have been expelled from college or who have never passed farther than through a primary school, have been trusted to approach the peasantry at such close quarters. Being generally self-seekers, and not particularly high-minded, they easily turned the peculiar position in which they were placed to their own advantage. The *pissar*, the interpreter of the law, and, more often than not, the only literate man in the district, could practically do whatever he chose. The elder, his nominal chief, in whom the word law inspired the same panic that it did in the breast of every other peasant, and who was quite bewildered by the bureaucratic complication of his new administrative duties, was absolutely helpless in the *pissar's* hands.

The elders could, however, find ample compensation for this kind of involuntary dependence, in the consciousness of the power they wielded over the rest of the villagers. At the present day they are really chiefs and masters. To the elders of both grades was granted the right of imposing fines, to the extent of one rouble at a time ; also the right to imprison or to impose compulsory labour, for a period not exceeding two days, on any member of their respective communes or *volost*. This "at their own discretion and without appeal," for any word, or act, or slight which they might consider derogatory to their dignity, such as omission to take off a hat before them, etc., of which there have been instances in recent times.

Neither with regard to the *mir* as a whole, may the elder's rights be lightly trifled with. In them is vested the exclusive right of convening meetings of the commune or the *volost*. A meeting assembled without their authorization is declared illegal, its resolutions void, and its conveners liable to severe penalties. By withdrawing from a meeting the elder can break it up whenever he considers that the debate is taking an unlawful turn. Thus the elder, though elected by popular vote, when once confirmed in his office becomes, for all practical purposes, the master of the body which elected him. A strange sort of local government certainly, though by no means an exceptional one under an autocracy. The local governments granted to our provinces in 1864, and to our towns in 1871, are modelled on exactly the same pattern. In both the chairman has more power than the body he presides over; an arrangement which has, as is well known, deprived both the provincial and the municipal governments of all vitality.

It is interesting to observe that in the villages the same trick did not produce this same effect. There the legislation met with an ancient custom of collective communal life and local government which no *ukaz* could uproot. True that in the last twenty years great corruption had crept in, even in the case of village government. But this was due to the internal economical decomposition of the village commune, which divided the inhabitants into two camps, the one composed of a knot of rich people, and the other of a mass of proletarians and beggars. The law then became a ready-made channel for the manifestations of the new anti-social elements, but not its direct cause.

So long as the process of the economical disintegration of the peasantry remains in an incipient state, as also in the thousands of communes which have until the present time preserved their original economical character, the bureaucratic prescriptions of the law remain a dead letter. The *mir* keeps to the traditional forms of local government. The elders, too, imbued with these traditions just as much as are their fellow-peasants, never think of making use of the strange powers reposed in them by the State. They remain in the subordinate and modest position formerly assigned to them—the "*mir's* men," to use our people's own expression.

It fared far worse with the other series of manipulations introduced into rural government, and which formed the natural supplement to those just dealt with.

Local village government had as yet to be linked in hierarchical order with the whole of the administrative machine of the State. After having created, in the midst of the once democratic villages, a sort of *tchin*, it was necessary to discover another *tchin* to which to subject the newly-founded one.

The government, in the honeymoon of its liberalism, acted with sense and discretion in entrusting this function to the *mediators*, officers nominated conjointly by the ministry and by the election of the citizens. These *mediators*, elected from among the liberal and really well-intentioned part of the nobility, exercised their authority with moderation and wisdom, not so much as regarded subjection to the control of the *mir*, which was perfectly equal to its task, but to protect it from the abuses and malversations of the local police and its *pissars*.

Since 1863, the year of the Polish Insurrection, which marks the point at which our Government adopted a policy of reaction, the state of things has changed considerably. The Government then threw all the weight of its authority into the scale with the party of the "planters," as the obdurate advocates of serfdom were, in 1861, christened. The whole administration changed sides, and Russia has since seen *mediators* who have used their powers in order to compel the peasants to gratuitously do all sorts of work on their estates; who have publicly flogged the elders—mocking at the law, which exempted them from corporal punishment, by first degrading them from their office, and then restoring to them the attributes of their dignity after they have been flogged.

The regular bondage of the *mir* began, however, a few years later. From 1868 down to 1874, when the office of the *mediators* was entirely suppressed, the *mir* gradually passed under the supreme command of the *ispravnik*, *i.e.*, the superintendents of the local police.

The peasants' bitterest enemy could not have made a worse choice.

A police officer—we are speaking now of the common police, charged with the general maintenance of order and the putting down of common offenders—is a *tchin* in the administrative hierarchy like all the others. But between him and a paper-scribbling *tchin* of the innumerable Government offices, there is as wide a difference as between a decent, peaceful Chinese, votary of his ten thousand commandments, and a brutal and fierce Mogul of Jenghiz—though both have beardless faces and oblique eyes. A police *tchin* is our man of action. With him the instrument of command is not the pen, but the fist, the rod, and the stick. He breaks more teeth and flays more backs than he issues papers. As regards other people's property, *tchins* of all denominations hold the same somewhat strange views. But whilst the scribbling *tchin* cheat and swindle, the police *tchin* ransack and extort like Oriental pachas.

In the villages, amongst the *moujiks*, who will suffer to the uttermost before "going to law," the police can afford to go to any extreme short of open homicide and arson. The function of tax collector alone, which, after the Emancipation, was entrusted to the police, offered a vast field for interference, abuse, and oppression, and of these the early *zemstvos* often complain. When the *ispravniks* were charged with the chief control of the rural administration, and could at their pleasure, and by way of disciplinary punishment, indict, fine, and imprison both the district and commual elders, self-government by the peasants, as such, was practially abolished. It could exist only as far and in so much as the police chose to tolerate it. "The *ispravniks*, thanks to the powers they have received, have transformed the elected officers of the rural government, the elders, into their submissive servants, who are more dependent on them than are even the soldiers of the police-stations,"—that is the statement made by the most competent authorities on the subject, the members of the *zemstvos*. (*Russian Courier*, Nov. 8th, 1884.)

The village communes have become for the country police a permanent source of income, often levied in a way which reminds one forcibly of the good old days of serfdom. Thus, in the circular issued by the Minister of the Interior on March 29th, 1880, we find the significant confession that, "according to the reports accumulated in the offices of the ministry," the country police officers, profiting by their right to have *one* orderly to run their errands, were in the habit of taking from forty to fifty such orderlies from the communes under their command, *whom they used as their house and field labourers*. In some cases the communes, instead of this tribute of gratuitous labour, paid a regular tribute of money (called *obror* by former serfs), amounting in some provinces, according to the same authority, to from forty thousand to sixty thousand roubles a year per province.

CHAPTER II.

THE *stanovois* and *ispravniks* are the menials of the provincial administration. Set over them are the Governors of the Provinces, with the Governors-General of regions containing several Provinces, both surrounded by a swarm of *tchinovniks*, attached to their persons, or grouped on "boards," "chambers," or "courts of justice" of various denominations. They do not come into direct contact with the *moujiks*, unless in exceptional cases, and by means of a few special officers.

In these higher grades of the administration, the chief means possessed by the servants of the public for enriching themselves at the expense of the peasantry assume a more refined form than that of petty bribery, and are at the same time far more profitable. They are the embezzlement of land.

I will pass over all the common everyday malversations of which the peasants are victims.

Those I will take as a matter of course; but I will devote a few pages to describing this peculiar mode of plunder because it is practised on the largest scale by the whole of the Russian official world, from petty clerks up to the Governors, Governors-General, Ministers, and courtiers, both male and female.

The Provinces of those vast oriental regions bordered by the steppes of Central Asia have grown particularly famous of late, by reason of the extensive and bare-faced embezzlement of the land. The land there is plentiful; the bulk of the population consists of alien tribes, who know next to nothing of Russian law or even of the Russian tongue, Russian being nevertheless the language in which all official documents are drawn up.

The *tchinovniks* are all-powerful here, and practically beyond control, so enormous are the distances from the Central Government. They can and they do profit by these opportunities, and permanently improve their private fortunes by robbing the people of the land, their sole valuable possession.

For the edification of those who indulge in singing pæans to Russia's mission of civilization to the barbaric tribes of Asia, it must be observed that these services are not without their drawbacks. The Russian advance in these regions presents two markedly different stages. The first, which follows immediately upon the conquest or the peaceful annexation, shows the Russian rule in a most favourable light. Order is established, slavery and brigandage disappear, as do also the distinctions of race ; laws are made equal for all, and respect to them enforced with severity tempered by justice. The best men of the Empire, such as Count Perovsky, Mouravieff of the Amour, Tcherniaeff, Kaufmann, in all of whom ambition is stronger than cupidity, are sent to administer the newly-annexed territories. They generally defend the natives as far as they can even against Russian officials, and the hosts of adventurers and swindlers who follow in the rear of a conquering army.

During this period the Russian settlers are almost exclusively peasants, who are invited and encouraged to migrate into the newly-acquired country, in order to give Russia a stronger footing there. The Russian *moujiks* never fail to answer to such an appeal. The word " free land " produces a magic effect on them, and they constantly stream in all directions where such treasure is to be found. Thousands of Russian villages have quite recently been founded on the Amour, on the enormous plains of Southern Siberia, among the Bashkirs, Khirghis, and Kalmuks of the Uffa, Orenburgh, and Samara Provinces, of which we shall shortly have to speak. Often the colonists precede the conquerors, penetrating into neighbouring countries scores of years before the armies. The annexation merely increases this movement. But in these parts land is plentiful—nobody suffers from the intrusion. The peasants take only so much land as they can till with their own hands, never appropriating one acre more. Furthermore, they rarely decline to enter into a friendly compromise with the natives.

Whilst the government of Siberia had to resort to the most drastic measures, such as the knout and hard labour, to prevent the nobility and rich merchants from converting the natives into slaves, the peasants of the Provinces of Astrakhan or Samara or Orenburg often paid a yearly tribute in money or in goods to the nomads whose lands they had appropriated. The rent in these districts is, however, so low, and the chances of receiving it so small, that neither the *tchinovnik* nor the capitalists feel tempted to acquire estates. The husbandmen of both nationalities have thus plenty of land for tillage.

The position changes when the increase of population has considerably raised the value of land and diminished the amount to be disposed of. By this time the province has become solidly incorporated with the rest of the Empire, requiring neither particular ability nor care in its administration. The men of talent, ambition, and energy are attracted to other fields. Their posts are filled by commonplace *tchinovniks*, who start a new mode of "Russifying" and "benefiting" the country—by taking the land from both the natives and their own countrymen, the Russian colonists, with perfect impartiality.

This spoliation of land is going on everywhere, even in Siberia. For this we have the testimony of Yadrinzeff, who is our best authority on Siberian matters; though in this enormous desert, covered with ice and marshes and impenetrable brush-wood, the plunder is of necessity confined to those few districts more thickly populated than the rest. On the Siberian main, with its one inhabitant to every three square kilometers—two square miles (English)—the land is as yet free.

The peasantry know of neither rent nor communal property: each husbandman takes as much land as he can find and can cultivate. But in other colonies and regions more favoured by nature the robbery of land is perpetrated on a very large, sometimes gigantic scale, and is the chief speculation of the *tchinovniks*, their relatives, and their hangers-on, as well as of their St. Petersburg protectors.

Thus in the vast provinces of Uffa and Orenburg, which together cover an area equal to that of the United Kingdom—the officials with their numerous retinue have, in the period between 1873 to 1879, by force and fraud embezzled no less than five million acres of the best arable land and timber wood of those districts.

The whole operation was carried out with all the appearance of legality, and was screened behind the plausible pretext of the "Russification" of the Provinces and "the improvement of their industries." With this object in view the officials asked and obtained permission to sell the land "unoccupied by peasants of any race," "on easy terms," to officials "who have merited such favour by their faithful services to the State."

As a matter of fact, only one item of that fable was true : the terms were the easiest imaginable, as excellent arable land, besides timber wood, which in these parts costs from fifty to one hundred roubles (a rouble is worth about two shillings) a dessiatine, were sold to the officials for merely nominal prices, varying from eight shillings down to tenpence a dessiatine, payable over long periods, varying from ten up to thirty-seven years. All the rest of the tale was an impudent falsehood and farce.

The land officially designated as free for occupation had generally been owned for generations, either by native *Bashkir* villagers or by Russians who had migrated years ago from the interior Provinces. It was precisely this fact which made these estates particularly attractive to the officials, as it enabled them to turn an honest penny. A certain Yusefovitch bought an estate of 1,017 dessiatines (a dessiatine is equal to 2·7 acres) for 4,804 roubles, and resold it to the peasants for 25,000 roubles. Another estate, for which 506 roubles were paid to the crown, was resold a few days later to the resident peasants for 15,000 roubles. A third Government official bought an estate for two roubles per dessiatine, and immediately let it to its occupants, at a rental of twelve roubles a year per dessiatine!

Of course but few of the peasants were able to pay such a heavy ransom for their own land. And for those who could not pay there was the sole alternative : either to be evicted or to accept a sort of serfdom, *i.e.*, to work gratuitously on the estates of their new landlords as remuneration for that small portion of land which he vouchsafed to leave in their hands. Thus was the bulk of the rural population of these Provinces almost totally ruined, reduced to beggary and indigence, and decimated by hunger.

In distributing these iniquitous gifts, the administration in most cases could not even put forward any services rendered to the State (*i.e.*, useless scribbling for regularly paid salaries) as a pretext. A private person, a teacher, who was not so much as a member of the civil service, paid nine hundred roubles for an estate which he immediately resold for 15,000. Two gymnasts bought each an estate of 1,000 dessiatines for 2,000 roubles, to be paid over thirty-seven years, whilst both relet their land at once for 900 roubles per year.

There was no limit to the favouritism shown

by the uncontrollable administration. A father received an estate of 6,000 dessiatines ; whilst to his daughters 1,000 each were allotted, and to his sons 2,000 each. The son married ; his wife's relatives were endowed with an estate. The next to marry was a daughter—her husband received an estate, and his family another.

The contagion of this land hunger spread far beyond the sphere of Uffa and Orenburg officialdom. Scores of *tchinovniks* flocked from St. Petersburg and other quarters, probably armed with good introductions, and, after having "served" in the Provinces two or three years received their rewards in the form of splendid estates of from two to three thousand dessiatines and upwards, in the most fertile parts of the country, on the shores of big, navigable rivers.

The Ministry of the Interior, then presided over by Count Valueff, at last grew jealous of the privileges enjoyed by the Governor-General who had such an Eldorado to dispose of, and ended by distributing estates on its own account to its own favourites. When the senatorial revision of 1879, called forth by all these scandalous corruptions, began its investigations, several of the highest officers of the imperial court and Government hastened to voluntarily resign their ill-gotten riches in order to avoid judicial proceedings.

It was rumoured that even the Minister of the Interior, Valueff, had had a finger in the pie. The reporters of German and English newspapers communicated news to that effect abroad, and the minister was indeed dismissed shortly after. The Russian press, however, in spite of this, received the following significant secret order, dated 4th October, 1881 :—" In some foreign periodicals it has been stated that Count P. A. Valueff has been implicated in the prosecutions now proceeding for misappropriation of land in the Orenburg region. The head board of management of the press department requests that the papers will not circulate, nor so much as mention these reports." Thus were these rumours suppressed without being so much as denied.

A no less conspicuous part in the wholesale peculation of land in the Uffa and Orenburg Provinces was played by the forcible or fraudulent "purchase" of land from the natives by the officials themselves, or with their active connivance. To show to what an impudent extent this legalized robbery was pushed one illustration will suffice.

In 1873 four local capitalists joined in purchasing from the Bashkir peasants 30,000 dessiatines of land, lying on the shores of the Uffa river, for the sum of 21,000 roubles, on condition that if it were afterwards found that there was more land in the estate than was specified in the agreement, they, the buyers, should have no further sum to pay.

(Such strange clauses as this are to be found in most agreements of this description, because the Bashkirs are easily cheated in the measurement of land.)

This agreement was, as usual, guaranteed by an enormous fine of 150,000 roubles. It was presented, as prescribed by law, for examination to the *mediator*, the immediate chief and protector of the peasants of his district, who approved of it and handed it on to head quarters, the Civil Board of Uffa, for registration. It was duly registered, and the four sharks formally invested with the right of ownership.

But at this point the Bashkirs "rebelled," and refused to fulfil their part of the engagement, and sent their men to lodge complaints in various quarters. After a "long series of charges," the Governor-General resolved to send a special Inspector to the spot to enquire into the case.

This Inspector chanced to be an honest man, who investigated the matter fairly, and reported: first, that the estate purchased comprised full 70,000 dessiatines; and secondly that it included splendid timber wood, which in these parts was worth no less than one hundred roubles a dessiatine. He discovered, moreover, as was natural, that the Bashkirs were quite unwilling to part with their property on such terms, and that the agreement to sell it had been extorted from them by threats, and under compulsion.

The *mediator*, their immediate superior, and the magistrate of the district, had ordered them to sign it, and had also arrested and removed from the village, "for disobedience and calumny against men in office," the twenty-four householders who had protested and absolutely declined to put their hands to the agreement. In conclusion, the Inspector reported that in acknowledgment of their services both the *mediator* and the magistrate had received small estates from their grateful clients.

The *mediators* and the *magistrates* were not the only officials who lent themselves to these disgraceful practices. Persons who held higher berths in the provincial government did the same.

Members of the Governor-General's Privy Council, who enjoyed the full confidence of the chief of the department, and through him held command over the police, "persuaded" the *Bashkirs* to sell their land to various persons on terms similar to those quoted above, and acquired on their own account about 30,000 dessiatines of land, mostly rich in timber wood.

A certain Shott, father-in-law of Cholodkovsky, chief of the Civil Service Department, acquired by similar "purchases" 50,000 dessiatines of land. Threats, extortions, imprisonment, and open violence were resorted to for crushing obstinate resistance. The officers most directly responsible for the protection of the peasantry from malversation and injustice, the *mediators* and the members of the Peasants' Court of Justice, had the largest share in this wholesale plunder.

A special commissioner, a General and chamberlain to the Emperor, Burnasheff, was sent from St. Petersburg in 1874 for the purpose of revising the Uffa Civil Board. He reported that everything was as it should be there. But it was afterwards discovered that he had himself "purchased" an estate of 20,000 dessiatines for 40,000 roubles in the Belebeef district, with the usual prescription of 80,000 roubles in case of the non-fulfilment of the agreement. This transaction was, however, annulled by the Senate in 1878.

The total number of agreements of this complexion registered by the Uffa Civil Board up to the time of the arrival of the Senatorial Inquiry Commission was one hundred and twelve; and the area of land covered by them was nothing less than one million dessiatines, or 2,700,000 acres.

The Senatorial Inquiry Commission sent into these Provinces by special order of the Emperor annulled some of the most scandalous of these legalized robberies, whilst some of the highest officials returned to the crown the estates they had received, declaring their ignorance of the injustice done to the peasantry who had previously held it. But the enormous majority of these land-robbers were not so sensitive about their reputations, and contrived to keep their booty. This has been revealed by the agrarian disturbances which occurred in these Provinces some three years later, in 1882, and which extended over four districts.

The Bashkirs of the Province of Uffa have been despoiled of their land definitely and irretrievably. The Governor-General, Kryshanovsky, who had headed the band of robbers, was dismissed; other officials got off with a "reprimand;" no one was indicted before a regular tribunal. Even this rebuke, however mild, was caused by the absolute want of discretion and moderation shown on the part of the robbers themselves, who in the fever of greed forgot all moderation and caution; and made the Uffa malversations a byword to the whole Russian Press.

In the neighbouring province of Samara, which lies on the left shore of the Middle Volga, and covers an area three times as large as Switzerland, the Administration has done exactly the same thing, without incurring any annoyance. The ethnographical and economical conditions of these two contiguous regions are pretty much the same, the northern part of the Samara plain, the Bagulminsk district, being chiefly populated by Bashkirs, the southern by Russian colonists, with a sprinkling of native Mordvas and Kalmuks, the latter mostly keeping to a nomadic state.

Twenty years ago the land was so plentiful in these parts that the peasants could rent from the crown or from the native nomads as much as they chose for from ten to fifteen kopecks a dessiatine. During the last twenty to twenty-five years things have gradually changed. The land was despoiled by officials and the private individuals whom they favoured. Up to 1881 the total amount of land thus abstracted from the Russian settlers amounted to about 700,000 dessiatines, or 1,890,000 acres. Enormous tracts of land were taken from the Kalmuks by means of sham purchases, more vile even than those practised upon the agricultural Bashkirs. The spoliation was effected gradually and cautiously, but the final result was the same. The Samara peasantry, prosperous in bygone days, is now one of the most wretched and hunger-stricken. Famine is of constant recurrence in this Province, the most terrible being those of 1878 and 1881, when, in some villages, one-fourth of the whole population died from starvation. In the same years millions of puds of corn were exported from the Province by the landlords, who battened on the land which had been robbed from the people.

If we skip the Province of Astrakhan, composed mostly of saline sands, where nothing can be got to grow and which are not worth robbing, we shall find ourselves in the Caucasus—the gem of nature, the country which disputes with the valley of the Euphrates the glory of having been the place chosen for the earthly Paradise of tradition. Our great poets and novelists, Pushkin, Lermontoff, Tolstoi, owe many of their best inspirations to the snowclad Caucasus, and they have all contributed to render familiar and dear to the Russians its sumptuous, grand, and grim character, as well as its noble, simple, and chivalrous inhabitants.

Nowadays, though as poetical as ever, the Caucasus has ceased to be the country of romance. Its warlike mountaineers are subdued; the country is peaceful; the Hadji Abrecks, the Kazbitchs, the Ismail Beys, the Abrecks, the terror of the valleys, are no longer to be met with there in living flesh and blood. These heroes of the poniard and scimitar have disappeared under forty years of uncontested Russian rule, and in the natural course of things have been supplanted by robbers, who may very possibly be as mischievous as they, but who certainly have nothing of romance or poetry left about them. The plunder of the State and of the people as regards their landed wealth (we will confine ourselves to this question here), by the Caucasian Administration and its *protégés*, combines the characteristics of both the Uffa and the Samara robberies.

It is as extensive and bare-faced as in the first-named Province, and as safe as in the last. The Caucasus is administered, not by a simple Governor-General but by a grandee of a much higher grade, a lieutenant who is, with rare exceptions, a Grand Duke, brother or uncle of the Czar. Nothing need be feared behind such a screen. Moreover, the dangers and difficulties of the conquest of the Caucasus, though they ceased to exist some thirty-eight years ago, still furnish a good pretext for the distribution of sinecures.

In this fabulously rich country the Government owns vast tracts of land, forests, mines of priceless value, and mineral springs classed under four hundred and eleven "heads" in the official list, which, however, bring to the exchequer next to nothing—at the outside an average of seventy-three roubles per estate. The reason for this is very simple: the greatest number, two hundred and fifty-five out of four hundred and eleven, are given to *tchinovniks* almost free of charge. In the Province of Kutais an estate comprising 2,000 dessiatines of arable land was let to a *tchinovnik* for ten roubles or, £1, a year. In the Viliet district of the same Province, 1,000 dessiatines of arable land were let to another man at a rental of twenty-five roubles per annum; and so on. (Slovo 1880, VII.)

During the same period, from 1866 to 1875, the administration disposed of about 100,000 dessiatines of land, from which its former inhabitants, the Circassians, had been expelled with fire and sword. Of this, 23,000 dessiatines were distributed amongst the military, and 26,000 amongst members of the Civil Service, whilst 50,000 were sold at merely nominal prices to a lot of speculators who obtained the protection of the administration.

In the vicinity of Baku lies the land containing the petroleum springs, which is valued at from 25,000 to 60,000 roubles a dessiatine. After the abolition of the power of sale by auction of some of the State revenue, this land was declared inalienable. Yet General Staroselsky, Prince Withenstein, and Prince Amilakhvary were each presented with ten dessiatines of this most valuable land. The Princess of Gagarine, wife of the Governor of the Province of Kutais, received five dessiatines of petroleum land, which she exchanged for 7,000 dessiatines of ordinary arable land in the

Province of Stavropol. Other five dessiatines of this same land were granted to the Princess Orbeliany. Full forty-five dessiatines were presented to the members of the Caucasian Civil Service for their relief fund. At the time to which all these statements refer, the short liberal respite of 1881, when the press was permitted to allude to such subjects, it was proposed to distribute the greater part of the forest covering the shores of the Black Sea in Abkhasia amongst the members of the Civil Service.

Our story will never draw to a close if we attempt to mention all that came to light in this question of land-robbery in the border provinces alone.

And how about the central provinces? Are the peasants dwelling there guaranteed at least against this form of oppression? Not quite,— though of course nothing like the wholesale theft going on in the border lands is possible here. In the interior, land is taken by instalments, a bit here and a bit there. The chief means employed to this end are legal chicanery and litigations, in which all the advantages are on the side of the great people, especially if they are members of the local administration. Since the Emancipation, hundreds of thousands of dessiatines have been filched from the peasantry by means of thousands of these lawsuits, which differ from open robbery only in name. The highest dignitary of the empire and the noble aristocrats themselves have not recoiled before such methods of enrichment. Count Dmitry Tolstoy, the minister, has despoiled the peasants on his Riazan possessions of their land; Count Sheremeteff is doing the same thing with the forty-two villages of the Gorbatov district, the inhabitants of which, to the number of 8,000 souls, were formerly his serfs.

The Tartars of the Crimea are still struggling for their strip of land with Count Mordvinoff. It is no uncommon thing for the despotic powers of the administration to be called upon to facilitate the success of these lawsuits. Thus, for instance, in No. 163 of the *Russian Courier* for 1881 we read that a peasant named Mikhailoff of Novosilka, a village in the Birutch district, Province Voroneje, was exiled by order of the administration to the province of Archangel. The offence alleged against him was that he incited his fellow-villagers not to pay their taxes. But the real facts of the case were as follows:

—the peasants of the villages of Novosilka, Podleska, and several others, had a lawsuit about some land with the neighbouring landlords, Sheglov, Sinelnikoff, and others. The peasant Mikhailoff was chosen by the joint village *mirs* as their delegate. He commenced operations with great activity, and discovered documents proving the injustice of the landlords' claims. They thought it advisable to have him removed.

Cases of downright robbery are not wanting either. The method generally adopted is, to forge resolutions of the *mir*, ordering that the coveted piece of land shall be yielded up. In No. 142 of the *Russkia Vedomosty* for 1881 the following curious incident is recorded. In the Fatej district of the Province of Kursk a certain lady, Nikitina, sold to various persons eighty-three dessiatines of land, which she of course stated to be her own, for two hundred and fifteen roubles a dessiatine. But when the new owners came to take possession of their property, they found it was occupied by the peasants of the village, Archangelskoie, who on hearing the claims of the new comers expressed the greatest surprise, and, flatly refusing to yield the land, drove away the intruders. At this Madame Nikitina applied to the *ispravnik*, who sent the *stanovoi* to the spot. This gentleman arrived at Archangelskoie, and having convened the peasants' *mir* began to admonish them not to offer rebellious resistance. The peasants answered unanimously that they had no desire to rebel against anybody, but that they would not give up the land, because it was their own, and they had never sold it to Nikitina, nor to anybody else, and knew nothing about the matter.

An agreement to that purport existed, however, dated 13th September, 1878, and was witnessed by a member of the Peasants' Court, who gave testimony to the effect that he had read this agreement before the *mir*, and was told that everything was correct, after which the deed was approved by the Peasants' Court, on 30th January, 1881, though it bore on the face of it the evidence of being a forgery. It did not bear the seal of the Archangelskoie *mir*, and it was signed by a total stranger to the village— the coachman of the member in question—and was witnessed as genuine by three servants of Madame Nikitina.

The *Golos* for the same year reported several similar cases as having occurred in the district of Balta, Province of Podolsk. Here the very men in office actually appropriated a good deal of peasants' land, by means of forged agreements, which the communal clerks drew up in the name of the *mir* by order of the *mediators*. One of the *mediators*, in virtue of such an agreement, received from the peasants *as a present* three hundred dessiatines of land, which constituted the only means of subsistence for a whole village. "It is easy to imagine," adds the correspondent, "the despair of the peasants when they were told that they had 'presented' the *mediator* with the only piece of arable land which they possessed."

Instances of such shameless abuses as these are, according to the *Golos*, numerous in the Province of Podolsk.

In other places, according to *Novoe Vremya*, the communal clerks drew up fraudulent agreements of this nature for their own benefit. In the Starobelsk district, in 1881, the Novoaidarsk Commune brought an action against their elder, Russenoff, for appropriating 1,000 dessiatines of communal land by means of a forged agreement (*Golos*, 1881).

These are a few specimens selected from among a heap of facts which the temporary relaxation of the censorship of the press has enabled the Russian newspapers to publish. Since 1882 we have heard no more of them, this class of publications being prohibited as inflammatory, and calculated to "disturb the public mind." They are considered seditious, and would involve severe punishment by the censorship.

With regard to the misappropriation of land, this is certainly not likely to diminish by the withdrawal of even this slight check.

The peasants are pretty nearly defenceless against the coalition of robbers. The official control is little more than a mere fiction. The central government depends necessarily on the information it receives from the *tchinovniks*, *i.e.*, the very accomplices or perpetrators of the robberies. And when some *tchinovnik* of good position, head of some board or governor of some province, is not actively compromised by the misdeeds of his subordinates, he screens them and conceals their actions none the less when once committed, because he is personally responsible to his superiors for all which happens within his jurisdiction. The all-directing, all-controlling Autocracy is a myth. The real Autocracy has long been broken up into a series of petty despotisms

—a sort of feudalism, which reproduces in modern Russia the same phenomenon discovered by the historical school of economists as existing in Western Europe in the middle ages,—the conversion of political power into economical predominance, of which the robbery of the land from the people is the most striking feature.

At the base of these operations, wherever committed, lies brute force. The Russian *tchinovniks* have at their disposal the military forces of the State, which they are free to use themselves, or to lend to any private person when needed, to put down any resistance which the peasants may offer to the appropriation of their land by any one of the methods described above.

Rebellions of the peasantry, followed by "military executions," having their origin in the embezzlement of land, can be counted by the score, though these events are rarely honoured with more than a short and dry notice in the newspaper chronicles of the day. Exceeding few are allowed to be thoroughly investigated and discussed. When some particularly gross abuse committed against the peasants forces itself upon the public notice and that of the higher ministerial circles, it is the deliberate policy of the government, ministers and Czar included, to hush the matter up as much and for as long as possible, because, taking the Russian reading and thinking public as it now is, nothing stirs it half so deeply as do affairs of this nature.

Among dozens of scandalous trials for bribery, embezzlement of the public funds, plunder in the Ordnance Department, etc., which the Government allowed to be heard in public, we remember only one important case—that of the Governor of the Province of Minsk, General Tokareff, and the man associated with him, in which the prosecution, followed by a public trial, was due to the initiative of the Government. Other famous "peasant cases," such as Count Bobrinsky's, Prince Sherbatoff's, etc., only came to light owing to some outrages committed by the peasants, who appeared as the prosecuted party, the Government exercising to the full its power over the press to prevent these affairs from being well thrashed out.

The Tokareff affair is a very instructive one, and is well worth studying for more reasons than one. It was tried before the fifth department of the Senate in November 1881, though the offence was committed in 1874. It took seven years to make its circuitous way to the court, and it was by a mere accident that it was not altogether swamped on the way. The trial only began in 1878, *four years* after the commission of the crime. The chief offender, General Tokareff, had by that time been promoted from the governorship of the Province of Minsk to the post of Special Commissioner of the Red Cross in Bulgaria, and was, together with his accomplice General Loshkareff, a member of the Ministerial Council. The third hero in the Loghishino affair, Colonel Kapger, had been created Knight of the Order of Vladimir, and he too was pursuing his noble career elsewhere. The trio would probably have been left unmolested to the present day had not two hostile parties at the court of St. Petersburg broken out into open strife.

The Trepoff-Shouvaloff-Potapoff Coalition, all-powerful at the court before 1877, received a severe blow by the Zassoulitch trial, which revealed Trepoff's infamous brutalities. His numerous opponents thought the moment most opportune for entirely crushing the coalition by a new blow and resolved to disinter the Loghishino affair, which would compromise several of the gang

Four years previously Potapoff, then Governor-General of the Lithuanian Provinces, had allowed his follower and subordinate Tokareff, then Governor of the Province of Minsk, to take several thousand dessiatines of land from the peasants of Loghishino. The act was committed under peculiarly aggravating circumstances, as the peasants struggled hard for their property. They "rebelled" several times, and were put down by a liberal allowance of flogging, but did not give up the fight. They lodged their complaint with the Senate, and after two years of litigation succeeded in 1876 in gaining their suit.

The Loghishino peasants, in so far as they recovered their property, were much more fortunate than most of their fellow-victims. They never thought, however, of taking further action against their former Governor for his past offences. But on this occasion Potapoff's adversaries, then in the majority in the ministry, became unusually alive to the people's wrongs. They brought the matter before the first department of the Senate. They fared badly in this, their first attack. The Senate, where Potapoff's party was probably well represented, opined that the affair ought to be concluded by a "reprimand" to Tokareff and his accomplices. Then the ministers discussed the matter at a cabinet council, and resolved to report the affair to the Emperor. The document wound up with the following remarkably bold and novel truth: "We consider it to be the duty of the Government to take severe and impartial legal action in cases such as this, of misdemeanour on the part of men in office." The Emperor's hand traced the word "certainly" opposite this sentence. Nevertheless the Potapoff party for three years succeeded in preventing the fulfilment of the Emperor's resolution. The affair was not adjudicated until 1881.

It was not in vain that the two hostile parties contended so bitterly—the one to bring it before the public, the other to hush it up. The details of the affair were sufficiently revolting to make it an ideal battering-ram. The Province of Minsk, of which Tokareff was Governor, forms a part of the vast region to which converged the greed of the Russian *tchinovniks*, until they discovered still richer prey in the enormous eastern outskirts of the empire. After the suppression of the Polish insurrection of 1863-64, the Government confiscated a total area of 60,914 dessiatines of land belonging to such landlords as had been implicated in patriotic conspiracies. These spoils of the vanquished the Government threw as prey to its officials, and especially to the bloodhounds who had helped to quench the insurrection,—as the hunter throws the remains of the skinned beast to his dogs.

This rich booty did not suffice to satisfy the appetites of the crew When the best of the landed property had been appropriated amongst them, the *tchinovniks* began to plunder the peasants, according to the common methods as practised elsewhere. One of these *tchinovniks* was the Governor of the Province of Minsk himself, General Tokareff, who obtained from the Governor-General of the region, Potapoff, an estate of 3,000 dessiatines, yielding an income of about 9,000 roubles a year, for the sum of 14,000 roubles, payable over twenty years. Tokareff's vassal, Sevastianoff, chairman of the Local Board of Minsk, carved out this estate for him from the land which belonged by right to the peasants of Loghishino.

It is evident that both Sevastianoff and Tokareff committed this act of flagrant robbery in full cognizance of the fact, though they denied it before the tribunal. The Loghishino peasants had been in possession of the land claimed by Tokareff from time immemorial, and had never paid an iota of rent to the Local Board. This could hardly be ignored by the Chairman of the Local Board, more especially as Loghishino is only twenty-five miles distant from Minsk. In addition to this, the peasants could show ample documental evidence in support of their rights, the best proof of which is the eventual success of their suit before the Senate in 1876: a charter from the King of Poland, and an *ukaz* confirming their rights from the Russian Senate. On being apprised of the impending transfer of their land to their Governor, they sent their deputies to the latter to explain to him how the matter stood, and at the same time forwarded the senatorial *ukaz* to Sevastianoff. The Governor, however, refused to listen to anything. As to the *ukaz* sent to Sevastianoff, it mysteriously " disappeared " at the office, and could never be recovered : in other words, it was stolen either by Sevastianoff on behalf of the Governor, or by his direction. When the Ministry to which the Loghishino peasants appealed, upon the failure of their applications at Minsk, applied for information at Minsk upon the subject, to the Minsk Local Government Board, Sevastianoff replied that the peasants' claims were void of any foundation, and that the land was unquestionably State property, and that therefore there could be no legal obstacle to its transfer.

The Governor-General himself did not lie idle. On learning that five peasants had been deputed to St. Petersburg to push forward the Loghishino suit, Tokareff reported to the ministry that these deputies were revolutionary agitators. They were accordingly at once locked up, and without further trial exiled to the northern Littoral, as is the custom in such cases with our Administration.

Having thus removed all obstacles, Tokareff was in 1874 formally invested with the rights of ownership over the Loghishino estate. But when he sent his agents to collect the rents the peasants refused to pay, and drove away the police. Twenty-six peasants were arrested and thrown into the Minsk prison. Tokareff's next move was to send small detachments of troops against the village to compel obedience and levy the money. The peasants, however, persisted in their refusal. When the troops were drawn up before them, they tried to force the line, but were driven back at the butt-end of the musket. The soldiers then fired a volley with blank cartridges, and withdrew without resorting to more drastic measures, the officer in command not being anxious probably to obtain a cross or promotion for the putting down of " civil enemies."

On the first news of the failure of the expedition—*four days before* the official report reached him—Tokareff hastened to telegraph to St. Petersburg that the Loghishino peasants had broken out into open rebellion and had repulsed the troops. Such a grave emergency requiring strong and prompt measures, the ministry sent a special commissioner from St. Petersburg, General Loshkareff, with most extensive powers. On October 25th, 1874, the General arrived at Minsk, received from Tokareff one battalion of soldiers, with 250 Cossacks, and marched against the " rebels."

In the subsequent, most revolting, part of the proceedings, the leading actor is Colonel Kapger, the *ispravnik* of Minsk, whom Tokareff attached to the expedition quite unlawfully. The duty of assisting the military in compelling obedience from the peasantry belonged of right to the *ispravnik* of Pinsk, Zolotnizky, because the Loghishino commune was in his district. Tokareff did not want to trust an affair of such personal interest to himself to the local police.

Kapger was under the circumstances a much fitter person, and was therefore attached to the expedition "as an experienced and capable police officer, to try and persuade the peasants to submit to the law," as the mealy-mouthed Governor explained in his own justification.

Kapger did not disappoint the expectations of his chief. His first precaution was to stow away in the Loghishino police-station (*stan*) several cart-loads of birch rods. When this order had been executed, he arrived on the 31st October at about mid-day at the village, and appeared before the peasants in the public square escorted by two policemen. He then began to abuse and vilify the villagers for their ill-behaviour, and announced that "an army was advancing on them, with a General who was authorized to bury them alive, to flog them to death, to shoot them, to do with them as he would with rebels,—anything he chose, if they would not at once submit."

The frightened people said they would submit, and hastened to send three deputies forward to meet and propitiate the terrible General. They met him at a few miles' distance from the village, and said that they submitted and would pay rent to General Tokareff. This did not, however, stay the advance of Loshkareff, who entered Loghishino at the head of his troops at night time, and immediately ordered the Cossacks to invest the village from all parts, "lest anyone might escape." A second deputation then came before him, bringing the traditional "bread and salt," in token of welcome and obedience. But the General said he would not accept these offerings from "rebels," until they had repented and fulfilled the claims of their landlord, who demanded about 500 roubles as a part of the rent for 1874, and 5,000 for the arrears owing to him for 1873.

This claim was a most impudent extortion. Tokareff had only been invested with the right of ownership in 1874. Any claim on the rent for the previous year was therefore absolutely illegal. On being questioned on this point by the tribunal, Tokareff explained that though he was formally invested with the right of ownership in 1874, still it had been reported to the chairman of the Local Board (his friend and accomplice Sevastianoff) that the Loghishino peasants were *informed* a year before by a *tchinovnik* of the Minsk courts of justice (who had neither juridical nor even administrative powers over them) that they must hand over one third of the harvest to

Tokareff. Then Stanovoi Trikovsky made a valuation, unassisted even by the local surveyor, and most generously adjudicated full 12,000 roubles to his chief, who reduced the sum to 5,500 roubles. Thus were the Loghishino peasants not merely robbed of their land, but had to present Tokareff with the capital which he had to disburse in the transaction!

The poor people could not, however, afford to ponder on the injustice of their case in the face of this array of bayonets and Cossacks. They submitted, pleading only for a short respite in which to sell some of their goods in order to make up the required sum. No respite was granted them. The General told them in firm but moderate language, as became so high an official, that they must collect and deposit in his hands the sum of 5,500 roubles within forty-eight hours, otherwise he would compel them to pay the whole sum of 12,000 roubles.

On this he retired, and shut himself up in the house assigned to him, leaving the command to the *ispravnik* Kapger. This officer went at once to the root of the matter, and showed to the full extent how " experienced " and " capable " he was in fulfilling the mission assigned to him by the

Governor. He refused to wait for the money even until the next morning. He rushed upon the peasants as one possessed, abusing them, calling them names, stamping his foot, boxing them on the ears, and shouting, " The rods, bring the rods ! I will flog you to death ! I will flay you alive ! "

He did not want the peasants to distribute the contribution demanded, according to their means. He made short work of all these formalities by assigning twenty-five roubles as the amount to be paid by each of the 233 households. Those who said they had not the money and could not pay at once were sent to the police station, and there flogged until they promised to find the money, selling their goods to the Jews of the village for a song, or borrowing from them the money at an interest of from one and a half to three per cent. *a week*. As the Loghishino peasants were poor people, according to the statements of the policemen themselves, many suffered very severely. One of the witnesses, the deputy Korolevitch, testified that the peasant Malokhovsky was beaten so savagely that he had never since fully recovered. He was a noncommissioned officer, and had only just returned from his regiment. He had had no time to get settled in his home, and was very poor. When summoned before Kapger, who was sitting at the police-station, he gave him full particulars as to why he was unable to pay the twenty-five roubles. He was conducted to the execution-chamber, and there flogged by two policemen under the personal superintendence of Kapger. After some time Kapger stopped the flogging, and asked whether he would bring the money or not. On receiving the same answer as before, he ordered the men to flog him once more. When he was again released, he said to Kapger that " whilst in the Czar's service he had never undergone the shame of corporal punishment." For this " impertinence" Kapger ordered him to be flogged for the third time. But even after that Malokhovsky brought no money, which was paid for him by the *mir*.

Lukashevitch, an old man of sixty-nine years, begged the *ispravnik* to give him a short respite, but the latter struck him in the face twice so violently that he could not keep his feet. Then he ordered him to the flogging-room, where he was flogged three times, Kapger telling his men to strike more heavily, and asking the victim whether he would bring the money now?

Many fainted under the ordeal. Kapger himself superintended the execution of the sentences, giving his men instructions as to how to use the rods so as to cause the victims to suffer more acutely. None were spared. The deputy Korolevitch testified to the fact that Kapger demanded the money even from a blind old beggar, Adam Tatarevitch, and when he said he had no money Kapger struck the poor fellow in the face, and was about to have him flogged; but Tatarevitch went to the village, and came back with ten roubles he had collected in Christ's name from his fellow-villagers.

The subordinates treated the people with the bestial brutality of invaders. A retired soldier, Chechotka by name, stated on oath that the *ispravnik's* men came to fetch him to the police-station in the dead of night, about twelve o'clock; that whilst he was dressing himself one Cossack struck his pregnant wife on the back with his horsewhip so cruelly that she fainted, and the next day miscarried.

By such means as these Kapger levied in two days the whole sum of 5,500 roubles, which were duly forwarded to the Governor. The troops retired, and General Loshkareff returned to St.

Petersburg, to report to the Emperor that order was restored in Loghishino, and that the rebellion had been put down without the use of fire-arms or *any violence*, thanks to the courage and ability of the *ispravnik*, Kapger, who had succeeded in persuading the mob to submit to the just claims of their landlord! Loshkareff was rewarded by the thanks of the Emperor, whilst Kapger was decorated with one of the highest military orders. (*Poriadoc*, 1881, No. 330-340.)

This is a fair sample of the truthfulness of the official reports, and the whole affair is typical of the style in which the military carried the law into effect. Of course such utter scamps as Colonel Kapger are rare, even in the ranks of the Russian police. Few *ispravniks* would strike a blind old man in the face, or take actual pleasure in the operation of flogging. But out of the seven hundred *ispravniks* and the two thousand *stanovois* of the Empire, there are hardly a dozen who during their term of service have not had to "put down" several of these "rebellions" amongst the peasantry, generated by the same feelings of despair, and subdued by the same methods of military pressure and wholesale flogging, as in the examples cited above.

CHAPTER III.

AFTER the beasts of prey—the vermin. Naturalists say that the most mischievous enemies of unprotected and primitive man are not the big carnivora with whom he has to fight now and then on unequal terms, but the lower forms of creation, —the insects, the mice, rats, wild birds, and other small pilferers, which overwhelm him by their numbers and omnipresence.

I will not venture to say that the same holds good with respect to the two classes of parasites which our paternal government has set on the *moujiks*. It is beyond doubt that both are extremely obnoxious. As to the question which of the two is the most so, it is rather difficult to give a positive answer.

The upper police and administrative officials— the *tchinovniks*—unquestionably commit enormous material damage among the people. But as they come into immediate contact with the peasantry on comparatively rare occasions, they cannot have much effect upon the moral side of the people's life. With the inferior police the reverse is the case. It must be granted that even as a question of finance they are a very heavy additional burden to the people. The 5744 *uriadniks* (rural constables) created in 1878, and constantly added to since, represent an outlay of 2,600,000 roubles a year, or about *twice* the sum the State Exchequer spends on primary education.

As every *uriadnik* extracts from the rural population subjected to him, by bribes, blackmail, and other devices, on an average at least twice as much as he receives in salary, the total cost of this amiable institution represents a good round sum, for which a much better use might be found than the support of this horde of blackguards. But monetary damages become almost trivialities by the side of the vexations, insults, petty everyday tyranny, and demoralisation which are poured into our villages by these guardians of the peace—unique of their kind.

To give the ring of truth to these strange statements, we have only to draw a sketch of these *uriadniks*, and how they came to exist.

When the Nihilist rebellion first burst forth, it assumed, as is well known, the aspect of a vast agrarian agitation in favour of the restitution of the land to its tillers. As the same aspirations, though obscured by the mists of monarchical superstitions, were smouldering among the whole of our agricultural class, the Government at once took the greatest alarm.

The fierce hunting of the Nihilist began through all Russia. The peasants did not rise in arms at the voice of the agitators, perplexed, bewildered by the unheard of appeal. But in the relentless chase after the Nihilists they kept aloof, and often assisted the propagandists to escape from the hands of their persecutors. The active part in the drama was played by the local officers of the State,—the police, the *stanovois*, the *ispravniks*, and the volunteer spies, who were furnished by the newly-born class of rural usurers, plunderers of the people and upstarts, who had fished in troubled waters. But in a well-regulated autocracy nothing can be left to private enterprise, least of all the craft of a spy. As to the local agents of the State police, they were so surcharged with so many other duties, and had under their supervision districts so vast, as to render an effective and minute survey impossible.

In 1878 a force of rural constabulary was created, and from that moment commenced the Babylonian captivity of the Russian peasantry to the police.

The *uriadniks* were created in order to strengthen the hands of the rural police, headed by the *ispravniks* and their assistants the *stanovois*. The *uriadniks* are therefore under the command of these officers, in their quality of general police agents. But like the gendarmerie created by the Emperor Nicholas I. for the benefit of the townspeople, their rural brothers are placed in a peculiar position.

The duties of the *uriadniks* are extensive and manifold. They are the masters of the village communes in the same sense as the governors are called the masters of their respective Provinces. Besides the function of chief of the communal police, they unite in their persons those of sanitary inspectors, inspectors of roads and buildings, and statistical agents, etc. They poke their noses into everything, prying into private households, and enforcing various prescriptions intended by the idle bureaucratic imagination for the benefit of the *moujiks*. Thus forsooth they must see that the peasant's house be ventilated and the windows opened, even during the winter time, when people have hardly fuel enough to keep the hard frost out of the door. To secure purity of air they are bound to prevent the keeping of manure in open courts near the houses, when in the whole of Russia not a single peasant, save a few German settlers, has an artificial dung-pit. The same solicitude for the stupid *moujiks*, who cannot feel the disadvantage of keeping cattle within their dwellings, inspired the prohibition of that bad practice, though the young cattle would otherwise be frozen in the courts, as the peasants have no warm stables.

Neither is the exterior of the village neglected. The *uriadnik* must see that the streets be kept clean, though in the villages there is no trace of a pavement, and the streets during the spring and the autumn, six months out of the twelve, are knee deep in mud. A lot of other equally benevolent and equally stupid prescriptions exist, relating to food, the construction of the houses, gardening, etc., all of which are fair examples of bureaucratic perspicacity and knowledge of the things with which they have to deal.

All this is amusing, but to an outsider only. To the peasants it is a very serious matter. The more absurd the order is, the easier is it for an *uriadnik* to convert it into a means of extortion and a source of abuse, owing to the exorbitant, the monstrous powers with which the *uriadniks* are armed in their quality of political bloodhounds.

Only a despotic government fully conscious of its many sins could in a fit of well-grounded fear put such powers into the hands of subordinate agents. They can enter anybody's house at any time of the day or of the night, examine everything, and question anybody as to any actions and purposes which may seem to them suspicious. They have the right of arresting and taking into custody any citizen of the district at their own discretion, without first obtaining any special warrant or authorization. The elders and the communal police are bound to arrest and to march off any prisoner at the bidding of the *uriadniks*.

Now let us ask, What are the moral and intellectual guarantees offered by these people, entrusted with such extensive powers over the liberty, honour, and property of their fellow-citizens? Whence does this horde of village proconsuls spring?

An *uriadnik* receives a salary of £20 a year, which, taking into account the cheapness of living in a Russian village, would represent from £40 to £50 at the English rate of value. We cannot therefore expect to see well-educated people in their ranks, quite apart from the aversion felt in Russia by all men of self-respect to the acceptance of any post connected with the police. Moreover, the considerable amount of physical exertion required from the *uriadniks* as a rule excludes the petty *tchinovniks*.

But as the *uriadnik's* duties imply a considerable amount of legal chicanery, they cannot be recruited at random from among simple folk, such as retired soldiers or non-commissioned officers. The *uriadniks* are chiefly picked up from among the dregs of the Government servants of the towns, and the outcasts of the intellectual professions : scribes out of employment, petty police-officers turned out of their posts for bribery or drunkenness, and so forth. In spite of this, this rabble, which had to be watched and watched like a host of pickpockets in a crowded room, were exempted by the Czar's government, to a quite exceptional degree, from any control whatever. The Russian press, as is well known, is not allowed to indulge over much in the exposure of the abuses and misdeeds of any of the members of the official hierarchy; but to attack a gendarme, a political spy, any officer connected with the defence of the autocracy against its civil enemies, is considered almost as a personal insult to the Czar.

The *uriadniks*, in their capacity of rural gendarmes, were on their creation granted the same immunity. The press was strictly prohibited from publishing any exposure of their vices. This fact, however strange it may sound, was publicly disclosed three years later by several Russian newspapers.

In the *Zemstro* newspaper of December 31st, 1880, the following details are explicitly given by the responsible editors: "At the founding of the *uriadniks* all possible care was taken to present them in the most favourable light to the public. To this end the *Official Messenger* and the official papers, which exist in every province, published, by order of the Minister, a number of reports tending to show their activity, sometimes put into the form of special narratives, sometimes in the form of statistical tables. Whilst, on the other hand, shortly after the law of 9th June, 1878 (instituting the *uriadniks*), had received due attention, namely, in September of the same year, the editors of all the newspapers and periodicals were ordered not to allow any censure of the activity of the police to appear in their respective columns, nor to 'discredit it,' by exposing any of its abuses. In case of the transgression of this order the delinquents were threatened with most stringent penalties. Thus did the *uriadniks* become quite inviolable to the press."

It may be added that the government defended these its Benjamins, charged with protecting it against agrarian revolution—even against their immediate superiors in office, the *stanovois* and *ispravniks*.

When this herd of 5,744 brutal invaders, scattered amongst the Russian villages, began their exploits, even the not particularly scrupulous law-abiding gentlemen of the police felt that they were bound to interfere. Numbers of *uriadniks* were turned out, or at least driven from one district to another, by way of disciplinary punishment. In order to suppress this flagrant proof of their worthlessness, the Minister of the Interior, General Makoff, expressed marked disapprobation to the police authorities wherever there had been frequent expulsions, "calculated to diminish the prestige of the *uriadniks* in the eyes of the peasantry." No wonder that the *uriadniks* grew so conceited with their self-importance that in the Province of Poltava, when one of them was fined eleven roubles by the magistrate, he flew into such a passion as to inveigh against the magistrate in open court, and to threaten him with a " protocol."

We have dwelt on these details at the risk of wearying our reader, because they prove to demonstration the fallacy of a very common prejudice concerning the Russian government. It is supposed that the educated class only are subjected to police tyranny. This is not so. Our government is free from any taint of partiality. Whenever it smells some danger to its own skin, all " the dear children," both peasants and the well-to-do, are dealt with on exactly the same footing.

The quite anomalous position created for these guardians of the public safety could lead to only one consequence. The *uriadniks* became the scourge of our villages, the terror of the peasants, the chief perpetrators of such violence and extortion as had never been heard of before. "Being perfect strangers to the village," says the *Zemstro* newspaper, "they despise the peasantry, as all upstarts do. They look on the rustics subjected to their control as invaders do upon a conquered people, on whom they may work their will. The extortions of the *uriadniks* in their insolence recall the rapacity of the soldiery. Not only are private individuals compelled to propitiate these *uriadniks* with bribes, but whole communes are saddled with illegal tribute. And such things happen not only in the remote corners of the vast Empire, but in the neighbourhood of St. Petersburg itself."

In view of these experiences, the *Zemstvos* have repeatedly petitioned for the abolition of the *uriadniks*. At the sitting of the St. Petersburg Zemstvo on 17th January, 1881, the deputies expressed their opinion in the following strong terms :—" the magistrates Volkoff and Shakeef do affirm most positively that the *uriadniks* are simply a nuisance to the people. They are doing no good, and are unable to do any good, being chiefly recruited from amongst half-illiterate clerks who are out of employment, and who take a distorted view of their duties." Baron Korf spoke to the same effect.

During the short Liberal respite of 1881 there was hardly one periodical, save Mr. Katkoff's *Moscow Gazette*, which did not pour out before its readers whole volumes of accumulated facts about the exploits of the *uriadniks*, varying in their nature from the too free use of the fist or whip to the most heinous and revolting crimes.

We will first open a page in the public career of a certain Makoorine, *uriadnik* of the Province of Samara, a jolly fellow, though somewhat excited and rough when in his cups. One fine morning, in the autumn of 1881, he arrived at the village of *Vorony Kust*, where a meeting was being held in the public hall. Here all his friends were met together, and amongst them Chaibool the Rich, a Tartar peasant. Having some business to transact with the *uriadnik*, Chaibool invited him, together with several common friends, to take a glass in his house. The meeting over, therefore, they left the hall in several cars. In opening the gate they let out a pig. The pig took it into its head to run after the *uriadnik*, though "Chaibool did his best to call it back." They crossed the village and reached the fields, the pig still running after the *uriadnik's* car, with the evident intention of escorting him up to the house of his host. The rural magnate took it as a malicious insult to his dignity on the part of the beast, and shot the pig dead.

After having taken their refreshment with Chaibool the Rich they returned back to the village a little elevated. There they met with a publican, the owner of the killed pig, who asked the *uriadnik* to pay for the beast.

At such audacity Makoorine lost his temper, swore, boasted of his official importance, and, according to the unanimous testimony of all the witnesses, said that "he, the *uriadnik*, had the right to shoot not only pigs, but men too, there being a law to that effect." A retired soldier, John Kirilow, who was present, observed that he also had served the Czar, but had never heard of such a law.

Without wasting words on his adversary, the *uriadnik* flew on Kirilow, knocked him down, and then dragged him into the court, and, calling his coachman to his assistance, struck Kirilow again.

The guardian of public order was, for this breach of the peace, condemned to six weeks' imprisonment; but as it was discovered that there were no less than *fifteen* similar suits pending against him, he was put under police supervision until such time as the verdict was pronounced on his accumulated offences.

Another *uriadnik*, that of Malo-Archangelsk, at the time of the Carnival arrived in the village, "drunk as a fiddler." On entering the public hall he behaved with gross impropriety. He cut the tablecloth to pieces with his sabre, and reviled the members with most opprobrious names. When some persons tried to get him to listen to reason he flew at them, brandishing his sabre, and drove them all, both guests and owners, out of the building.

In Ivanovka the *uriadnik*, on entering the house of a peasant to make an inspection as to whether it was kept clean, saw a young calf tied to a table leg in the kitchen. At such slovenliness the *uriadnik* lost his temper, and after having reviled the women who were spinning in the other room, as best he could, he drew his sabre and cut the calf to pieces.

In Poroobejka an *uriadnik* came upon a woman making dough. She was in a hurry to make the bread for her household, and had left the floor unswept. Exasperated by this negligence, the *uriadnik*, after giving the woman a severe scolding, overthrew the kneading-trough before the woman's eyes, and upset the dough on to the dirty floor.

In Dmitrovka the *uriadnik* Lastochkin met a wedding procession, going with songs, according to custom, from one relative of the newly-married couple to another. He ordered them to disperse at once, though the elder of the village was amongst them. One of the guests, Basily Kareff, remonstrated against such interference, explaining that they were celebrating a wedding. The *uriadnik* as his only answer struck Kareff twice with his whip.

The crowd got into a rage; they flew at the *uriadnik* and handled him roughly. He would, perhaps, have fared yet worse had he not taken refuge in the parson's house.

On hearing of the disturbance the whole village assembled round the parsonage, clamouring to have the *uriadnik* delivered up to them, and it was only thanks to the soothing influence of the parson that the *uriadnik* escaped lynching A protocol was drawn up about the "insult offered to the *uriadnik*," and Kareff was condemned to seven days' imprisonment.

All these examples, given by eye-witnesses to a correspondent of the *Zemstro* newspaper, refer to one small district alone. None of them are of any particular importance, but they contain much local colouring, and convey a pretty fair idea as to the moral physiognomy and distinctive attributes of the new type of our village magnates.

In one place the *uriadnik* fired into a crowd of unarmed people; in another charged a crowd busied in quenching a fire, on horseback, with sword and whip. In a third case, a freshly built peasant's house was demolished, under the pretext that it was not constructed "according to the regulations." In a fourth, the *uriadnik* assaulted and inflicted severe bodily injuries on a church-warden, for not having appeared before him with sufficient alacrity when sent for.

In the Bogorodsk district the *uriadnik* was in the habit of stealing the peasants' oats for his own horse by night. When caught on one occasion in the act, so far was he from being put out of countenance that he threatened the owners with imprisonment, and then, having sent his errand-boy to fetch his sabre and revolver, declared himself to be engaged "in the execution of his duty," and triumphantly made his way through the assembled throng. The *ispravnik*, on receiving complaints from the peasants, ordered the *stanovoi* to investigate the case. The accusation proved true, but the *uriadnik* was not even discharged, and continued to hold his office as guardian of the public safety in peace.

In one of the towns of the Province of Poltava, during fair time, the *uriadniks* formed themselves into a body, which wandered through the town, and amused themselves by tearing off the earrings and necklaces of the peasant women who came to the fair adorned in their best national attire, alleging that the national costume had been prohibited by the Czarina's *ukaz*.

We will close this list, which might be prolonged *ad libitum*, by mentioning some of those cases where these rural despots, accustomed to impunity, have given vent to their low instincts in acts which recall the worst features of the days of serfdom.

In the Mogilev district of the Province of Podol, Daniel Yasitsky, the *uriadnik* of the village Chemeris, after having for a long time and with impunity distinguished himself by the extortion of money from the innocent, and blackmail from such thieves as were caught in the act, whom he was in the habit of setting free by his own authority,—this Daniel Yasitsky indulged in the following practical joke.

By threats and blows he compelled two of his subordinates, peasants' "decurions," to harness themselves into a car and drag him to the town of Bar, distant about four miles. Yasitsky was simply dismissed.

Another still more revolting case was tried before the St. Petersburg tribunal, April 23rd, 1886.

Gerassimoff, the *uriadnik* of the village Borki, in the Peterhof district, was convicted of having subjected several peasants to *the torture* in order to extort from them confessions about a robbery committed by unknown persons. A peasant named Marakine, and two brothers of the name of Antonoff, were all three kept hanging for several hours on a sort of improvised strappado. Stripped of their clothes, and barefoot, their hands were tied behind their backs by a rope, which was then passed over a rail, fixed high up in the wall of an ice cellar. The bodies of these unfortunate men were then raised above the level of the ice ground, which they could hardly touch with the tips of their toes.

The *uriadnik* now and then appeared, requesting them to confess, and dealing them blows on the head on their refusal to comply with his wishes. One of the three victims, the peasant Marakine, on the way to the torture-chamber was subjected to other treatment no less infamous. The testimony of the elder of the village is particularly characteristic. "Gerassimoff the *uriadnik* came to me and asked whether I could lend him thirty men. 'For what purpose do you need so many?' I asked. Then he answered, pointing to Marakine, 'I mean to make this fellow run the gauntlet.'" To this the witness made reply that he would never permit such things to be done to the peasants of his commune. Then Marakine's hands and legs were tied, and he was fastened by the legs to the back of the car, his body on the ground. The horse was then made to run, and Marakine was dragged in the mud for about ten yards. Then Gerassimoff said to the elder, "Bring me some straw, we will burn him a little," but witness refused to bring it to him.

Gerassimoff was found guilty, and sentenced to *one year's* penal servitude. So lenient is the Russian law towards crimes *against* humanity, reserving its ferocity for those who are working on behalf of humanity.

Such barbarities, which, had they been committed by a Turkish officer, would have set European diplomacy on fire, are of course exceptional, though it would be illogical to suppose them unique.

From the opposite end of the Empire we hear of things which are no better, indeed, if anything, rather worse. It was proved by judicial inquiry before the Kisheneff tribunal, that in the Orgheef district the *uriadnik* and the communal authorities had for a long time used various instruments of torture in their judicial proceedings. One of these, called *butuk*, figured on the table of "material evidences" in the court. It is a wooden instrument, composed of two sliding beams, which serve for screwing the feet of the culprit between them. These abominations were not unknown to the police. The matter was, however, only brought before the tribunal because the authorities arrested the wrong man, on whom they used the *butuk* with such cruelty that the victim was crippled for life.

The patience of our people is great; too great, indeed, but not unlimited. Since the *uriadniks* have been introduced the number of so-called offences against officials in the execution of their duty has considerably increased amongst the rural classes. The first official statistics bearing upon the subject show, for instance, that in 1877-81, in the district included under the St. Petersburg jurisdiction (embracing several provinces), the peasants form 93 per cent. of such offenders, whilst the privileged classes supply only 7 per cent. In the Kharkon region the former furnish 96 per cent., the latter only 4 per cent. in the rural districts, of such offences; all refer to the *uriadniks* or to the rural *stanovois*. Thus, to the lawlessness of the police must be accorded at least the merit of instructing our peasants a little in the art of taking the laws into their own hands, which may, perhaps, ultimately serve some useful purpose.

HARD TIMES.

CHAPTER I.

THE outcry for more land was the first sound the ears of educated Russians were able to catch, in the confused din of voices which rose from the masses below. Our *moujiks* were never tired of repeating the same requests again and again.

It was in vain that the Government, in order to satisfy their greed after land, offered them various cheap makeshifts. The *moujiks* displayed a stoical indifference to these advances, and went on endlessly repeating the same refrain about land.

What could be supposed to satisfy the peasants more than the condonation of the arrears in the taxes? or the reduction of one rouble per head of the annual land-purchase payments? But even to these offers the peasants turned a deaf ear. When spoken to about the condonation of the arrears, says Enghelhardt, they would answer: " The solvent payers will only regret their former punctuality—that is all. Condonation or no condonation, those who have nothing can pay nothing. The present arrears condoned, fresh ones will be made next year, since they cannot pay." They will point to such and such villages which are not in arrears and are in no need of condonation, " because they were not wronged with regard to their land."

As regards the reduction of the land-purchase money, they showed the same wooden insensibility. " One rouble per head," they said, "mounts up to a large sum of money to the crown, but to us separately it is a trifle, hardly perceptible at all. We *moujiks* are quite ready to pay our dues, if only we can have more of our dear land."

The land is the object of the peasant's day-dreams and longings, as well as of a touching, almost filial respect and devotion. In the peasant's songs and in their ordinary speeches the usual epithet applied to it is " mother," or " little mother." The whole tenor of peasant life in Russia suggests the idea that the chief aim of their existence is to serve the land, and not to use it for their own advantage.

The Russian *moujiks* are, as a rule, quite unconcerned as to what is called "comfort." They seem to consider a Spartan mode of life, and indifference to hardships, a good deal in the light of an attribute of man. In Eastern Russia and the Volga Provinces they scoff at their neighbours, the peasants of Tartar origin, who are fond of soft bedding and dainties, and who ride in longshafted buggies, which rock them as a cradle might, instead of suffering their bowels to be jolted out in the traditional Russian *telegue*. I will not cite as an example the life of the poorer class of peasants. Amongst them privations are unavoidable. That which bears particularly on our present object is the life of such peasants as could afford to live quite comfortably if they chose.

If you enter the house of a notoriously rich peasant, whose granary is brimful of corn, who keeps half-a-dozen horses in his stables, and who has probably in some remote corner under the floor a jugful of bright silver roubles, laid aside against a rainy day, you will be surprised at the extreme simplicity, nay squalor, of his household arrangements. All peasants, the rich as well as the poor, live, with very few exceptions, in the same narrow peasant's *izba;* these homesteads presenting a square of fifteen to twenty feet in length and width. Into this space, divided into one or two rooms, both children and grown-up people are all huddled together. The quantity of air afforded for respiration is so puzzlingly small that our hygienists are forced to admit the endosmical action of the walls as the only hypothesis which will account for the fact that these people are not literally suffocated.

"Furniture" is a word which can be used only in its broad philosophical sense when applied to the dwellings of these people. They really have no furniture beyond a big unpolished table of the simplest pattern, which stands in the place of honour, in a corner under the *ikons* or images of saints; and some long wooden benches, about two feet deep, running all along the walls. These benches are used for sitting on in the daytime and for sleeping on at night. When the family is a large one, some of its members, at bed time, mount on to the upper tier of these shelves, which run all along the upper part of the wall, like hammocks in a ship's cabin. Nothing bearing the likeness of a mattress is to be seen; a few worn-out rugs are thinly spread over the bare wood of the benches or on the floor, and that is all. The everyday coat, just taken off, serves as a blanket. Beds are a luxury hardly known, and very little appreciated by the Russian *moujiks*. Even in the peasants' hotels, the *dvors* on the chief commercial highways of the interior, frequented by the rich freight-carriers, a plentiful and luxurious table is kept, but nothing but bare benches in the way of beds are to be found. In the winter the large top of the stone oven is the favourite sleeping-place, and generally reserved for the elders, so that they may keep their old bones warm.

All the peasants dress in pretty much the same manner, which is extremely simple,—no undergarment; a shirt of homespun tick or of chintz, sometimes of red fustian—this last is very much appreciated—and light cotton or linen trousers. The richest wear boots, which are used by the poorer sort only on great occasions. The " bast " shoes, which were used in the middle ages in Europe, and have since disappeared, are in common use among the bulk of the Great Russian peasants. In the winter, a kind of home-made woollen boot is preferred, and the long woollen homespun coat is replaced by a sheepskin overcoat, by rich and poor alike. The peasants wear this fur dress the whole year round, rarely taking it off unless when at work or asleep. Being so seldom changed, the peasants' clothes are not a model of cleanliness, but both men and women, as a rule, keep their bodies very clean. Every family which is not totally destitute has its hot steam-bath, where all wash, on the eve of every holiday, with great punctiliousness. The poorer amongst them, who have no bath of their own, use the family oven for this purpose, just after the removal of the coal. This is a real martyrdom, as the first sensation of a man unaccustomed to such exploits is that of being roasted alive.

As to the food, which forms the chief item of expenditure to people living in a simple way, and which presents the greatest scale of variation among peasant families, the allowance which has to be made for wealth is exceedingly modest.

Those peasant families which can be classed as rich or well-to-do use wholemeal bread and gruel all the year round, and eat it to satisfaction. But as long as they keep to the "peasant's state" —in other terms, as long as they are living from the land and tilling it with their own hands— the Russians do not depart from the chiefly vegetarian and extremely simple system of diet common to the average peasant. They eat meat on Sundays, and occasionally on a week-day, never every day. It is a general maxim amongst all peasant households not to spend anything on themselves if they can help it that is not " home-made," home-grown, or reared on their own premises. As no family, living by husbandry alone, can rear on its own premises a sufficient number of cattle to supply it with meat every day, it, as a matter of course, adopts the above-mentioned custom.

It does not spring from stinginess. The same families, when moving to a town and engaged in business, spend just as much and live in just the same style as the well-to-do merchants and townspeople. But, so long as their ties to the land remain unbroken, the land is their first care. Very close-fisted in his household expenditure, the rich peasant will yet spend generously for the extension of his agriculture, the improvement of his working implements, or the augmentation of the number of his cattle. He expects a good return for his outlay, as the contrary would be proof of a blunder on his part. But money is not the only thing he has in view : he is heart-sick at the sight of bad crops, without in the least thinking of the possible pecuniary losses. If quite well off he will none the less overwork himself at the hay-harvest, just as much as will the poorest man in the village.

There is, indeed, a good deal of unselfishness in the intense love borne by the peasants to the soil, which we townspeople, living in almost complete estrangement from nature, can hardly realise, but which is deep-rooted in the heart of every *moujik*— nay, of every husbandman—without distinction of nationality. The same feeling as that which inspires our peasants' poetry, breathes in the monologue of Alexander Iden, squire of Kent, overlooking his garden before John Cade drops in. Michelet, in his well-known prose poems, has sung the ardent love of the French peasant for his " mistress " the land.*

* I quote this beautiful passage as translated by John Stuart Mill (*Pol. Ec.*, p. 172).

"If we would know the inmost thought, the passion, of the French peasant, it is very easy. Let us walk out on Sunday into the country and follow him. . . . I perceive that he is going to visit his mistress.

"What mistress?—His land.

"I do not say he goes straight to it. No; he is free to-day, and may either go or not. Does he not go every day in the week? Accordingly, he turns aside, he goes another way, he has business elsewhere. And yet—he goes.

"It is true, he was passing close by; it was an opportunity. He looks, but apparently he will not go in; what for? And yet he enters.

Yet everything in men bears a national stamp, which reflects the historical and social peculiarities of their native countries. Alexander Iden—a man living amidst the turmoil of feudal struggles, who has found on his small estate a safe refuge, alike from the necessity of being an oppressor and the wretchedness of being oppressed—experiences in the fact of possession a quite different enjoyment from that of the peasant painted by Michelet, who, an owner above all things else, has recently come into the possession of a freehold estate into the bargain. It is yet another thing among our *moujiks*, with their perfect abhorrence of the idea of private property in land, and the peculiar agrarian arrangements which are the result of this objection.

"At least, it is probable that he will not work; he is in his Sunday dress: he has a clean shirt and blouse. Still there is no harm in plucking up this weed and throwing out that stone. There is a stump, too, which is in the way; but he has not his tools with him, he will do it to-morrow.

"Then he folds his arms and gazes, serious and careful. He gives a long, very long, look, and seems lost in thought. At last, if he thinks himself observed, if he sees a passer-by, he moves slowly away. Thirty paces off he stops, turns round, and casts on his land a last look, sombre and profound, but to those who can see it, the look is full of passion, of heart, of devotion."—(*The People*, by J. Michelet).

There is no strip of land in Russia—save, perhaps, that whereon the peasant's house stands—which the peasant can call his own in the same sense as a continental peasant proprietor or English freeholder can claim land. To-day he holds one piece of land—by to-morrow a redistribution is voted for by the *mir*, and he receives another piece, which may be larger or may be smaller than the first, according as to whether his family has increased or decreased in number, but which certainly will lie in some other part—or better, parts—of the common field. We say parts because the families never receive their allotment of land in one whole block, but in a number of small plots and strips, scattered sometimes over ten, fifteen, or even more, localities, and changed every two or three years. This plan has its inconveniences; but the peasants prefer such an arrangement. It affords room for perfect fairness in the distribution of this most precious commodity—the land—which always presents great variety as to the quality of the soil, and its position with respect to the roads, the village, the water, etc.

Under such an arrangement there was no room for the development of the jealous and exclusive passion of ownership, so characteristic of small holders, and little room indeed, if any, for attachment to the communal field as a whole, where each peasant wanders with his own plough and scythe. The cohesion between the men always proves stronger than their attachment to the soil.

Thus our peasants have no difficulty whatever in migrating to new places, provided they may start there on the same work and in the same mode of life which has proved itself congenial to them in their old homes. It may be said, without exaggeration, that most of the peasants in the thickly populated central provinces of Russia are permanently on the look-out for some new settlement. As a rule, before moving, the peasants send forward their explorers—the *khodoks*, or "pedestrians," and await their report about the new country.

Not rarely it happens, however, that vague rumours about the fertility and abundance of free land in some far-distant province set dozens of villages in motion, which sell their goods, put what can be transported into cars, and start on their journey without any further inquiry, and generally end by paying dearly for their childish rashness. On the other hand, it must be mentioned that in no case do the peasants migrate by isolated households, as do the American settlers in the West. A peasant never detaches himself, unless compelled by main force, from his village and his *mir*. Whether well pondered or not, the migrations are always made, either by whole villages or by parts of villages, considerable enough to form a new village commune, a new *mir*, at the new place. Of the many thousands of peasants who, on being compelled to abandon the ploughshare for a time, find regular and tolerably remunerative employment in the towns, nine out of ten return to "their villages" and the hardships of a peasant's life so soon as they have amassed a sum of money sufficient for the purchase of a new instalment.

In our peasant's longing after land there is more of the love of a labourer for a certain kind of work which is congenial to him than of concrete attachment of an owner to a thing possessed. A *moujik* will survey with great complacency the furrow his plough and his faithful friend his horse have traced. At the sight of a golden cornfield his heart will be filled with exultant joy; he will delight, strong man as he is, in the powerful exertion of mowing. But to fallow land, the land which is no more an active participator in agricultural labour, he will probably be quite indifferent. Certain it is, that he will not, like Michelet's peasant, covet such land with wistful, passionate eyes on his Sundays, when he has to abstain from working on it; nor would he, in going off, turn round to throw at his mistress "a look full of passion."

Moreover, if his neighbour has little land and a big family he will, at the *mir's* bidding, give up a part of his land for his neighbour's sake, without in the least feeling as if a part of his own flesh were cut from off his body.

It is not exactly the land, the given concrete piece of land, which a *moujik* loves—it is the mode of life which the possession of land allows him to live, and which blends into one inseparable whole both the work and the men in whose company he is accustomed to toil. This feeling, because it is less individualised and more complicated, is none the less intense; perhaps the reverse is rather the case. A Russian *moujik* probably feels much more grieved and downhearted at being separated from his furrow than does a husbandman of any other nationality.

Uspensky, in one of the many sketches drawn

from life which we owe to his powerful pencil, has well caught this double characteristic of our peasants' longing after their land. In his "Ivan Afanasieff" he shows us a peasant in whom, as we shall see, this feeling developed to an almost morbid intensity, and the tragedy of whose life consists in the necessity for constantly violating it.

"Ivan Afanasieff, peasant of Slepoe Litvinovo, in the province of Novgorod, is a sterling example of a genuine husbandman, indissolubly bound to the soil both in mind and in heart. The land was in his conception his real foster-mother and benefactress, the source of all his joys and sorrows, and the object of his daily prayers and thanksgivings to God.

"Agricultural work, with its cares, anxieties, and pleasures, was so congenial to him, and filled up his inner life so completely, as to exclude even the idea that husbandry might be exchanged for something else—for another and more profitable employment. Though Ivan Afanasieff is by no means enamoured of the land, as the reader might have concluded, he is yet so closely united to it, and to all the mutations which the land undergoes in the course of the year, that he and the land are almost living as parts of the same whole·

"Nevertheless, Ivan Afanasieff does not feel in the least like a bondsman, chained to the soil ; on the contrary, the union between the man and the object of his cares has nothing compulsory in it. It is free and pure because springing spontaneously from the unmixed and evident good the land is bestowing on the man. Quite independently of any selfish incentive, the man begins to feel convinced that for this good received he must repay the land—his benefactress—with care and labour.

"With these pure, conscientious principles to form the base of the whole existence of a genuine, unsophisticated peasant family, the germ of a wonderfully high moral standard of life might have been sown amongst them had they been allowed to thoroughly develop these fruitful ideals of free unconstrained union, based on the unshaken conviction that good must be earned by good. But alas! though Ivan Afanasieff and his foster-mother—the land—are doing their respective duties with most scrupulous conscientiousness, times have come which seem to set no value on either the purity of these relations, or on the fact that they form the backbone of the moral strength of the whole Russian peasantry.

"'Money!' roar the new times, granting neither exemption nor respite. 'But for pity's sake! how can I leave the land?' supplicates Ivan Afanasieff. 'Suppose I go and seek some other employment for the sake of earning money, why then the land will be neglected, and we have lived all our lives by the land!'

"Ivan Afanasieff is so devoted to husbandry, is so genuine a *moujik*, that the highest salary he might obtain would not allay his craving after land, after the various sensations and appearances which surround the labours of the husbandman, and connect his soul and his mind with the sky and the earth, with the bright sun and the gorgeous dawns, with the storms and the rains, the snowdrifts, the frost, the thaw—with all God's Creation, with all the wonders of God's Universe.

"'Money!' roar the new times, and willing or not Ivan Afanasieff begins to struggle to scrape together some roubles?"

As Ivan Afanasieff had a horse, which, according to his own account, "though a poor, spare jade, dragged its feet along nevertheless," and an uncle whom, by dint of prayers and supplications, he induced to lend him ten roubles for three months, he resolved to try his luck in trade.

He did not prove a success in this, his new calling, because he had not the hawker's stuff in him; he was unable to swear that his wares had cost him three times as much as they had done, calling God and all the *ikons* of the Virgin Mary to witness to his truthfulness; nor did he know any of the tricks by which to preserve himself from dangerous competition.

After a lot of trouble and much anxiety, Ivan Afanasieff was happy to be able to return what he had borrowed from his uncle. "From this time forth no—God forbid! Never will I try commerce again. When I returned to my uncle the money he had lent, I felt relieved as from a heavy burden. No! let us not meddle with this commerce. It is no business for us peasants."

The whole last ten years of Ivan Afanasieff's life is fraught with similar incidents. Being quite devoid of cunning and craft—for agricultural labour teaches no such lessons—Ivan Afanasieff fails in all enterprises which have money-making as their aim.

"A relative of his," we resume the quotation, "employed as a nurse in St. Petersburg, procured him a situation as a *dvornik* (porter) in a house. He spent all his money on his railway ticket and arrived at St. Petersburg. But he was as frightened as a child at the sight of the ant-hill of 'strangers' which he beheld around him. He was frightened, too, at his dry, uninteresting work, done for the sake of money; he found it hard, too, to work, away from 'his own people.' He lost his place owing to his half-heartedness, and had to make his way home again on foot, penniless, begging in Christ's name, until, half-starved, he reached his native village, distant three hundred versts from the capital.

"'Then I could repose at last to my heart's content,' he said. 'Leave all these places alone! Henceforth will I prefer to live on dry bread so long as it is in my own home.'

"On his return to his nest after every such absence, Ivan Afanasieff feels an almost childish joy, though he is always worse off than when he started. He is glad to have a crust of bread, provided it is home-made, and that he is allowed to live amidst his own home surroundings, and with people whom he knows and loves.

"'Money, money!' roar the new times, and Ivan Afanasieff, who has none, is entrapped once more in some financial enterprise. He is engaged to dig a canal near Lake Ladoga. They give him ten roubles in advance, and promise more, besides board and lodging. Ivan Afanasieff could not but accept; but lo! at the close of some six months he returns home again without money, without health, without clothes. It turned out that he and his companions had to sleep on the snow, that they were fed on carrion, and cheated most shamefully as to wages; that a multitude died from various diseases, and were buried in hot haste anywhere. After having passed through all these ordeals and seen the heart-sickening sufferings of others, Ivan Afanasieff is glad to run away, with his passport as his sole remuneration. And how pleased he is with his thatched roof, his big stove, and his diluted acidulous 'home-made' *kvas!*

"However exhausted and toil-worn he may be, the life in 'his country,' and especially the return 'to the peasant state' and to agricultural labour, speedily wipe out all traces of illness, of sorrow, and indignation from his face, which once more looks calm, noble, benevolent." — (*Uspensky*, Vol. vii.)

CHAPTER II.

No greater misfortune can befall a peasant than to become a landless *batrak*, compelled to hire himself out to landlords or to his rich fellow peasants. The *moujiks* make, indeed, but a slight distinction between the state of a slave and that of a hireling. "To hire yourself out is to sell yourself," they say; and they feel the same abhorrence for the state of a hireling as a freeman feels for the state of slavery. There is no name more opprobrious for a peasant than that of *batrak*.

"Oh, they live in clover," these *hen poachers* (popular *sobriquet* for the policemen) said to Enghelhardt a *moujik* friend of his, a genuine, passionate husbandman of enormous physical strength, and cleverness and ability in the management of his farm.

"Why, would you take such a place yourself?"

"I take such a place?"

"Yes."

"No, God forbid! I would not be a *batrak*."

Another day several peasants from a neighbouring village came to his stores to buy some bushels of corn.

"Why do you not buy it from your landlord?" he asked.

"Our landlord!" they exclaimed. "What kind of corn can you expect him to have when he is a *batrak* himself?"

"And what contempt there was in these words!" adds Enghelhardt. The landlord being a poor man served as steward to the estates of his rich neighbour.

It must be observed, however, that these same *moujiks* never neglect an opportunity of turning an honest penny by their labour, if it in no way implies permanent dependence. Even the rich *moujiks*, who have plenty of food and everything they require in their homes, after they have harvested their own crops, and during the winter months, when there is no field work, most willingly accept any work they can get on the landlord's fields or farms. They do not in the least consider it to be derogatory, nor would they call themselves on that account either *batraks* or "hirelings." They hate permanent engagements only as implying dependence on the pleasure of a master, because a *moujik*, even though he be poor,—provided he lives by the labour of his hands, on his own bit of land, without applying to anybody for assistance,—is an independent, self-confident man, enjoying his ample share of human dignity and self-respect.

It stands to reason that the ideas of personal dignity held by our *moujiks* are not the same as those held by the people of the civilised countries of Europe. When meeting a "gentleman" or an official, no matter of what grade, the peasant will take off his hat and stand bareheaded when spoken to. If anxious to express extreme gratitude to any one, he may perchance bow down to the ground, as grown-up children bowed to their parents in the families of the middle classes up to the present generation. The *moujiks* do not consider any of these acts to be humiliating, holding still in this respect to the same standards of ideas as have prevailed in all countries, modern and ancient, when just emerging from the patriarchal state. Yet they possess in a high degree one qualification which in all centuries and in all lands has constituted the very essence of human

dignity—they are truthful. There is neither false
hood nor deceit in their lives. In their families,
and in all their mutual relations, everything is
clear, genuine, frank ; this is true, even as regards
egotism and brutal oppression. There is much
harshness in the everyday life of the peasant,
but millions of our people have lived from
generation to generation without knowing or
suffering a lie.

"That which struck me most," says Enghelhardt, "when I was listening to the peasant's
discussions at the village meetings, was the
freedom of speech the *moujiks* granted to themselves. *We*" (he means the well-to-do, the upper
classes), " when discussing anything, always look
suspiciously around, hesitating whether such or
such things may safely be uttered or not, tremb-
ling lest we should be collared and taken before
some one in authority. As to the *moujik*, he fears
nothing ; publicly, in the street, before the whole
village, he discusses all kinds of political and
social questions, always freely and frankly speaking
his mind about everything. A *moujik*, 'when not
in disgrace with his landlord or with the Tzar,'
which means that he has paid all his taxes to
both, is afraid of nobody. . . . He may stand bare-

headed before you; but you feel that you have to deal with an independent, plainspoken man, who is not at all inclined to be obsequious to you or to take his tone from you."

Rural Russia fought bravely and pluckily for the preservation and freedom of its husbandmen, endeared to it for so many reasons.

From the first, however, it was quite evident that all the odds were absolutely against the peasants. With plots of land so small that the best-conditioned half of our rural population (originally "State peasants") could only win from them sufficient to supply one-half of their yearly income, whilst their poorer brethren (former serfs) could only gain from one-fifth to one-third of the amount absolutely needed for food and taxes; with a burden of taxes for the State peasants equal in amount to 92·75 of the entire value of the annual produce of their allotments, and for the former serfs about double that proportion— 198·25,—I say, that with such an arrangement as this, for the peasants to live on the profits of their land was an arithmetical impossibility.

The State peasants had to provide, as we have seen, for about 40% of their annual expenditure by some other means, whilst the former serfs had to find, some two-thirds, others four-fifths, of their yearly income from outside sources. In cases where this is found to be feasible, the taxes imposed on them would absorb, as we have seen in a former chapter, about one-half (45%) of the yearly gains of the people on their land and elsewhere, kindly leaving for their subsistence the larger half (55%). This is practically a permanent *corvée* of about three days a week paid in money. To call this a "tax" is a flagrant abuse of the term ; but our peasants would not quibble about that, for these *moujiks* are wonderfully ready tax-payers.

They would freely give up three days of their week without a murmur, or so much as asking for an account, and would go merrily on their way with the remaining three, if only they might employ them also on the land. In other words, if they had their plots of land enlarged, so as to be able to draw from them the whole of their exceedingly modest revenue, they would be content. As, however, their bitter outcry for more land was never listened to, they have had to make the best shift they could. With their peculiar adaptability, which never despairs and which puts a good face upon all difficulties that cannot be avoided, they left no stone unturned in the endeavour to make both ends meet. They applied for whatever work they could hope to get, and adapted themselves to any they could find : in the factories, at the railways, at the wharves, in the thousands of petty trades which congregate in towns.

The whole of the peasantry being in extreme need of extra earnings, it is a difficult matter to find employment for all in a non-industrial country like Russia. Every trade is overcrowded.

The sums realised by "outside" (*i.e.*, non-agricultural) employments are very considerable. In the Provinces of Novgorod one-third of the peasants are permanently engaged in various outside industries, their wages amounting to about nine and a half millions of roubles a year, whilst from their land they receive only two and a half millions. Out of this total of twelve millions the Novgorod *moujiks* pay 65 per cent. in taxes. In the Province of Yaroslav, where about half of the whole population is engaged in outside employments, the non-agricultural revenue brings in eleven and a half millions of roubles a year ; in the districts of the Province of Tver the peasants earn on an average about eight roubles a head by extra work, or about one and a half millions a year.

The losses, too, are enormous, especially in the

agricultural branches of the "migratory employments"—the most important of all. There is neither system nor order; and there can be none in these wholesale wanderings of people in search of employment.

The peasants of the Province of Viatka rush to Samara, whilst those of Samara try their luck in Viatka, and both Samara and Viatka send batches of their men to the Black Sea steppes, which return them a Roland for their Oliver. The travelling expenses, and the losses occasioned by the hundreds of thousands of failures, amount to scores of millions of roubles every year, and are a direct loss in the popular economy, acting on the peasants as a dead weight, which drags them downhill.

To atone for these constant and unavoidable losses our people have but one expedient—increase of work. They have reduced to the extreme limit the number of able-bodied labourers kept on the land so as to set a greater number free for the chances of "outside earnings."

The petty trades carried on by artisans, who work at home—*kustary*—have flourished from of old in the villages of Great Russia, as a supplement to agricultural work.

At the present day the hard exigencies of commerce have gradually compelled a considerable number of these artisans—husbandmen—to give up husbandry altogether and to devote themselves exclusively to their trade. But the bulk of them are still tillers of the soil, dedicating only the winter months to their trade. They make all kinds of goods which do not require expensive machinery for their manufacture: earthen, steel, iron, leathern wares, woollen, cotton, and linen stuffs, carts and harness, hats, furniture, mats, carpets, lithographs and *ikons*, ropes, musical instruments, candles, soap, glass, beads, bronze, and silver finger and ear rings; they bring up singing birds, they knit laces, they hew grindstones,—they do everything which a ready mind, coupled with a hungry stomach, can suggest. Invention and ability make good the extreme deficiency of tools, as well as the complete absence of any assistance from scientific technology.

In the finest specimens of these wares the workmanship is brought to remarkable perfection.

The Inquiry Commission mentions that most of the goods of some of the best commercial houses of Moscow, trading in Parisian silk hats and Viennese furniture, are manufactured by these *kustary* peasants in their villages. The Podolsk laces, and the linen of Kostroma, belong to the best specimens of these articles. The crushing competition of large factories working with machinery, and the swarms of usurious jobbers, have together, by steadily cheapening the products, driven these small artisans to lengthen their hours of labour to a frightful extent.

Amongst weavers, lace-makers, rope-twisters, fur-dressers, and locksmiths, it is a common thing for men to work for seventeen hours a day; sometimes more.

The mat-makers—an extensive trade, by the way, carried on in four hundred villages of twenty-six provinces, and returning two millions of roubles yearly—have to work such appallingly long hours that they invented a sort of relay system which, as far as we know, is quite unique of its kind. They sleep three times in the twenty-four hours at about equal intervals: first at dark, until 10 P.M., when they awaken for their night's work; then after the early breakfast at dawn, and again after the dinner-hour. As they work, eat, and sleep in the same dusty workshop, and certainly fall asleep as soon as they drop on the floor, they contrive to squeeze out of themselves nineteen hours of work a day, and sometimes twenty-one! "When the work is very pressing," says the report of the Commission, "the mat-makers do not sleep more than three hours"—one hour at a time.

Among all these trades, in which millions of people—men, women, and small children—are engaged, there are few in which the working time is less than sixteen hours a day. The result of all this fearful toil, which absorbs every hour unoccupied by field labour—*i.e.*, the whole of the winter and part of the autumn—is, that they barely manage to pay their taxes, and do not starve. This is what is meant by "peasants making both ends meet."

After such horrors, field labour may well assume the guise of recreation. Yet the peasants when ploughing "at their leisure," because this is not pressing work, rise before the sun and do not go to rest until it is dark, reposing but for a short time during our very long northern day. As to the harvest-time, it is not without cause that in our peasants' idiom it is called *strada*, or "sufferance."

Strange! the medical inspectors say, about most of our factories, that the hygienic conditions under which the "hands" work are so bad, and the hours so long, that the only thing which prevents their being slaughtered in a mass is the fact that they return to their villages for the summer months, and are there able to recuperate their strength. Exactly the same conclusion was come to by the Commissioners concerning many of the *kustary* mat-makers, fur-dressers, and others: they are able to go on, solely because it is only during the winter months that they work under such fearful pressure, and till their plots of land in the summer.

At the same time all those who have written about Russian village life—nay, all who have ever spent a few holiday months in a Russian village —know that it is difficult to conceive of more exhausting work than that which is performed by the peasants during the "sufferance time."

When mowing the hay (on their own land, of course) the peasants do not allow themselves more than six hours' rest out of the twenty-four. Towards the close of the harvest season the peasant gets thin, and his face grows dark and emaciated from overwork. "They get so exhausted that, if the fine weather lasts for a long time, the peasant will in his secret heart pray to God for rain, that he may have a day of rest. In fine weather the peasant, however weary, will never desist from his labours. He would feel ashamed.' (Enghelhardt.)

Of course I do not say this as disproving the surgeon's opinion as to the strengthening effects of agricultural labour. Certainly it is the healthiest of all occupations, provided only that the labourer has food enough to make up for the great physical exertions this work entails. I only wish to show that our peasants do not spare themselves, either behind the *kustar's* stand and the factory loom, or on their land ; that their capacity for work is at least equal to their power of endurance ; and that they really do their utmost in the terrible struggle for life and independence which they have been waging under such unfavourable conditions for the last twenty-six years.

It cannot be said of them that they have won the battle ; yet neither are they defeated. Certainly they have saved their "honour" and something more.

The bulk of our peasantry, that is to say, about two-thirds of it, have preserved the land and the position of independent husbandmen to which they are so passionately attached; and for its possession they continue to pay, in some cases, the whole, in others twice the value of what it yields in taxes, twisting themselves with miraculous dexterity out of the clutches of usury, and from under the hammer of the tax-collector. But in spite of this they are gradually giving way. Slowly, it is true, obstinately defending every inch of the ground; sometimes retrieving in a good year that which they lost in a bad one; but, on the whole, losing their foothold unmistakably, fatally.

Those frightful figures, showing the increase of general mortality, are there in all their barren eloquence to attest this fact. The Government returns regarding recruits prove that insufficiency of food, combined with over-work, begins to produce its baleful effect on the health of the rising generation. The peasantry, as a whole, lives in greater want than it lived ten—nay, fifteen years ago.

The scientific study of the daily fare of ordinary peasants—which means those who are rather badly off—would, in all probability, prove a no less puzzling problem than to calculate the average quantity of respirable air inhaled by each, and would inspire a high opinion as to the marvellous adjustability of the human stomach.

When in 1878 some people brought samples of bread from the Province of Samara, nobody in the Geographical Society would believe that it was intended for the consumption of man. It looked like a brownish, sandy coal of inferior quality, or like dried manure; and it fell to pieces when pressed between the fingers, so great was the quantity of non-nutritive ingredients mixed with the flour. This, of course, is exceptional; but the average peasant family in our villages leads a life of privation and fasting, which would do honour to a convent of Trappists. They hardly ever taste meat. Whole-meal rye bread, and whole buckwheat, and gruel made of grits, are dainties which they only taste during the few months, sometimes weeks, which immediately follow the harvest.

Children from these families, when placed in situations in town as domestic servants, in well-to-do households, at first literally over-eat themselves on ordinary sifted rye bread, as other children might do on cakes.

In the prisons the convicts banter and tease one another. "You rogue, you! Look how you have fattened on the Crown's *chistiak!*" which means whole-meal bread; because in the prisons rye bread, though of inferior quality, is dealt out without any extraneous admixture, whilst the ordinary run of villagers, during eight months out of the twelve, eat bread mixed with husks, pounded straw, or birch bark.

It is when reduced to such extremities as these that the peasant "puts himself in harness," to use the *moujiks'* colloquial term, for applying to the ruinous assistance of the local usurer. He cannot help it if his children cry for bread. "They are not like cattle, the children," said one peasant, apologising for his insolvency. "You cannot cut their throats and eat them when there is no forage for them. Willing or unwilling, you must feed them." And the peasant then steps on to the slippery declivity, at the foot of which yawns the abyss of misery and degradation, which is summed up for our rural population in the one word "*batrak*." A whole third of our peasantry has slipped down this descent since 1861, and is now at the bottom. There are twenty millions of landless rural proletarians in modern Russia. Among the remaining forty millions, who still hold their land, there are yet other millions who will join the ranks of the ruined to-morrow if not to-day. Here is an extract from the reports of a Commission of Inquiry, giving a detailed and graphic account of the economical position of such peasants as are on the high road to become *batraks*, though nominally they are still landholders. I translate literally, in the endeavour to preserve the ingenuous tone and style of the original.

"*Pankrat Horev* and wife have a family of six daughters and one son, all under age. He is the only full-grown workman in the house. He pays taxes for two souls—*i.e.*, two shares of land. His property: 'one cow, one horse, two sheep.' Their means of subsistence: 'know no trade. Have ground their last sack of oats.'

"*Ivan Jdanov*. Family of five people, with one full-grown workman. His property: one cow, one horse, one sheep. Means of subsistence: 'no bread since the autumn. Begs with his children. In order to pay off the second instalment of his taxes has sold his hay.'

"*Fedor Kazakovzev*. Family of six people, with one full-grown workman. Pays for one and a half souls (share of land). His property: one cow; no horse. Means of subsistence: no trade, goes begging. To pay the taxes has sold his stable.

"*Emelian Jdanov.* A family of ten people, of which only one is a full-grown workman. Pays for one and a half souls. His property : no cow, no horse, the house in ruins—uninhabitable. Means of subsistence : begging. To pay the taxes has sold his last horse.

"*Efrem Tarasov.* A family of six people, with one full-grown workman. Pays for two souls. His property: one horse, old and lean, one sheep. Means of subsistence : no bread, are begging.

"*Evsignei Usskov* has a family of six. Pays for two souls. His property : one horse, one calf. Means of subsistence : are eating their last oat bread. To pay the taxes has sold his pig.

"*Procl Jdanov.* A family of seven people, with only one full-grown workman. Pays for three souls. His property : one horse. Means of subsistence : to pay the taxes has sold his house ; to buy bread, his cow. This they have already eaten, and now are begging.

"*Andreian Zaushnitzin.* A family of seven people, with one full-grown workman. Pays for two souls. His property : no horse, no cow, two sheep. Means of subsistence : to pay the taxes has sold his horse and his cow. No bread, are begging. And so forth, and so forth. . . . '

("Records of the Zemstvo of Orloff District in the Province of Viatka," 1875, page 254).

For peasants in such an evil plight, whose name is legion, to be converted into downright *batraks* would be to a certain extent a deliverance. They would no longer be worried about the taxes, and their position would be clear once and for ever. That which makes them cleave so tenaciously to the land is the hope, but rarely realised, that "perhaps" by some lucky chance they may be able to struggle through their present straits, rear their children, and then, when the household numbers several workmen, all will be well again, and they become "real *moujiks*" once more.

Hundreds of thousands of peasants, when once compelled to resign the land, leave the country altogether, swelling the masses of our town proletarians, paupers, and tramps. The bulk of the landless peasants do not, however, leave their native villages. They seek employment as *batraks* in the village or neighbourhood, and wander as day labourers from one master to another. Their families live in the village, in the *izba* (cottage) they have retained, and to which the father returns when out of employment.

If the commune is not very hard up, no taxes or duties are imposed on these *bobyls* and *bobylkas*, as the male and female landless householders are called. In such communes as are in distressed circumstances, and which cannot afford to exempt any, they have to bear their share of the common burdens, such as the digging of wells, the construction of bridges, or, if they keep any cattle themselves, the hiring of the communal shepherd.

But, whether they pay anything or not, whether they work or beg, the *bobyls* and *bobylkas* retain their full voice in public affairs and their place at the communal meetings of the *mir*. There is not a single case on record of any attempt on the part of a *mir* to curtail these rights, which, in their opinion, is due to manhood and not to property. It is not, however, to this class, which is so absolutely dependent on the *koulaks*, and so easily cowed by them, that the *mir* can look for an active support in its struggle for freedom against its chief enemies and oppressors.

There are few rural districts which enjoy real and genuine self-government. In most of them the Government appointments are monopolised by *koulaks* and *mir*-eaters pure and simple. An honest peasant, a *mir's* man, anxious to protect the *mir's* interests against the village *koulaks* as well as the police superintendents, stands but a poor chance against one of the *koulaks*, supported, as they are, by the police and local administration. To obtain the post of *starshina* for their own man, or to overthrow some notorious swindler hated by all, who may chance to fill it for the time being, the peasants have to resort to no end of canvassing, agitation, and diplomacy, in order to detach from the *koulak* who opposes them some influential supporter of his own set, to inspire the timid with courage, and persuade them to firmly resist the threats of the "*stanovoi*," the "*ispravnik*," and the "*member.*"

More often than not these efforts are not crowned with success, and hence the fact that there are few districts in which there is no underhand contest going on between the commonalty and the board of officials. But in a prosperous and truly agricultural commune—which is tantamount to saying in a strongly united commune— the *koulak*, even when accepted as the head of the administration, will think twice before committing a gross injury to a member of the *mir*, or before plunging his grasping hand too deeply into the communal cash-box. For a flourishing agricultural commune, not in "arrear" with its taxes, even the police has no overpowering terrors, and the *mir* grows very obstinate when provoked beyond a certain limit.

We gaze on another picture when we look at poor half-ruined villages, swamped by "arrears," overcrowded by *bobyls* indebted almost to a man to the *koulak*, and dependent on his kindness and mercy. Here the *koulak* reigns supreme. Whether in office or not he is absolute master of the position, because he is able to sway the *mir's* vote at his pleasure. Both elders and judges, who among other powers have the right to inflict corporal punishment on the peasants of their district, are the tools, friends, dependents, obedient to his biddings. In such communities the *koulaks* verily are absolute masters. The very vastness of the powers wielded by the *mir* makes it extremely dangerous to resist the *koulak*; should there be no rivalry among the set, almost impossible.

Thus are the *koulaks* not merely instrumental in the material ruin of our peasantry; they are the chief agents in the demoralisation and perversion of our people's public spirit, and of those democratic communal institutions which first fostered it. At the same time the *koulaks* serve as a channel by which the demoralising influences, which come from the police and the administration, are infiltrated into the hearts of the villages.

CHAPTER III.

BETWEEN these two classes—the rural proletarians on the one hand and the rural plutocracy on the other—stands a third, that of the "grey" *moujik*. In their ranks we place all peasants who, without being necessarily free from debt to the *koulak* or to the State, have, nevertheless, preserved their land, their agricultural implements, and their cattle in good working condition, so as to have a reasonable hope of retrieving their position within an appreciable time. Excluding all such merely nominal land-holders, who have no cattle wherewith to till their land, we shall still find this to be a sufficiently numerous class. At the present time it counts among its numbers certainly more than one-half of our rural population, though it is constantly on the decrease. The upper stratum melts into the rural plutocracy, the lower swells the ranks of rural proletarians.

This is the class which forms the backbone

of Russian strength; it intervenes between the State and bankruptcy; it upholds the great popular principles of social and economical life, and struggles undaunted against the police and the tax-gatherer; it withstands the heavy pressure of the rural plutocracy; it resists the downward influence of the proletariats.

It must be in fairness admitted that in defending their political and social principles our peasants, the "grey *moujiks*" at their head, have shown the same tenacity and obstinacy as they showed in the protection of their favourite economical status. Indeed, they have succeeded in preserving in absolute integrity the fundamental axiom that there shall be no such thing as personal proprietorship in land or in any other source of wealth which is provided by nature. Notwithstanding the many influences working in an opposite direction, they still hold, with a few unimportant exceptions, to the principle that a man has a right of ownership in a thing only in so much and in so far as it embodies his labour. In politics they stick to the idea of the supreme authority of the *mir* and of the perfect equality of its members, considering the many violations of these principles as abuses; and

against them the popular conscience never ceases
to protest.

There is certainly a far greater uniformity in
the popular mind as to these two fundamental
points than might have been anticipated from the
diversity in the social condition of the people.

The very *koulaks* and *mir*-eaters who misapply
them to their own ends will generally recognise
them in the abstract. That which in our social
organisation had become damaged, vitiated, corrupted, is the interior relations between the
members of the commune, affecting the opinions
held as to a man's moral conduct and his obligations towards his fellow men. This ideal of
"unity," then, which we have endeavoured to set
forth in one of our former chapters, was the
natural outcome of the material and social equilibrium existing at one time in Russia, but which is
now gradually disappearing from our village communities.

The village in its natural state—as it was in bygone days, and could yet be under a more rational
agrarian arrangement—may be best described as
an association of labourers, amongst whom there
are no conflicting interests to check or mar that
sentiment of mutual good-will which is inherent

in all men as social beings. Friendliness amongst these peasants was assured by their not being in any sense competitors: that which in other branches of industry can be attained only by means of a complicated social arrangement is obtained in agriculture by itself. I mean independence of the market. Each lives by the fruit of his labour, not from the profits he might or might not get by selling to somebody else. Two husbandmen tilling their fields side by side are not rivals, unless in the noble and artistic emulation that may be felt by two labourers delighting in their work. The failure of the one can in no way be considered by the other as a windfall for himself. Nor could one feel grieved, or in the least alarmed, if the other, being stronger or abler, or simply luckier, earned more

Differences in wealth always existed among our peasants. In each village there have always been rich families, poor families, and those of moderate means, a difference regulated by their respective ability and industry, and particularly by the number and age of the members which formed each household. Large families, composed of five, six, and even more full-grown workers, and " rich families " are synonymous terms even now. But as for every pair of willing hands there was land waiting to be tilled, a diligent peasant could well afford to be indifferent to the question as to how many silver coins his neighbour had hidden away in his strong-box. He was in no need of it; and in the next generation the chances of birth and death might make his family a large one, and make him in his turn a " rich " man. Labour was the certain source of prosperity and independence. It was also an all-sufficient ground for self-respect and for considerate treatment from his fellow-men. Labour became, to a certain extent, sanctified in the eyes of the people.

"God loves labour," say our people, though nowadays there are few who attach more significance to these words than to many other virtuous precepts handed down by popular tradition. Men belonging to the type of unselfish workers are rare in our time. Lukian, for example, "the *batrak* of Ivan Ermolaeff, with whom even his exacting master was satisfied, was an exceptional man." He believed labour to be meritorious before the face of God. "God loves labour," he often said, and believed it firmly. With a view to future beatitude, he moved logs and carried beams, rolled stones, and over-taxed his strength over the most back-breaking efforts, not only without a grumble or any feelings of spite, but with an unshaken belief that all this was agreeable to God. " He likes it! " said Lukian, whilst, red as a turkey cock and dripping with perspiration, he was pulling up an enormous stake sticking in the bed of the river under the direction of Ivan Ermolaeff. He was all wet, he was sighing and groaning from the strain ; but God saw these efforts and approved of Lukian. The stake creaked and splashed as it was pulled out of the deep mire of the river's channel, and Lukian then knew for certain that " God had seen his efforts and had added a new mark to the many he had already gained by his labours."

In losing the power to secure the satisfaction of the people's needs, labour lost much of its dignity, scope, and attractiveness. The only thing which is appreciated now, and which alone can secure to the peasant peace, safety, and respect, is money. But from daily observation and experience he soon learns that money cannot be viewed in the same light as the product of the land. The people who succeed in making the most money are not always those who work the hardest, but in many cases those who do not work at all, and are only the more respected for being idle, both in the wide world outside, of which the *moujik* catches occasional glimpses, and in the village where he lives. The *koulak*, whose motto is " Only fools work," is certainly the man whose position is the most enviable. Nobody would dare to lay a finger on him. To him not only the small fry—*starshina, pissars, uriadniks* —but the *stanovoi* himself are kind and considerate. The "grey" *moujik* cannot help feeling tired and disgusted with his eternal drudgery over his "cat's plot," which brings him in such a pittance. He also longs to be safe, and not to live in momentary dread of a flogging; he, too, wishes to be respected, and would not in the least object to being courted. The greed for money now permeates the whole rural population; they all join in the mad chase after roubles, a chase which moreover diminishes their attachment both to the land and to the village.

On the land a household works together; the product is the result of common labour, and is considered as common property. The *mir* as a whole plays an all-important part in the cycle of agricultural life, as guardian of the land, meadows, and forests, controlling their fair distribution amongst the people, and directing the common work. When making money in towns, everybody depends on his own personal ability and industry. The village does not in any way assist or protect him, and the household very rarely does. His duties towards the *mir* become a burden to him, and he is much tempted to resent the constant drain on his resources made by his own relatives.

This is one of the chief causes of the breaking up of the large patriarchal families, which flourished among the Russian peasants in olden times. " The Gorshkovs," says Uspensky, " were one of the richest and largest families in Slepoe Litvinovo; in proof of which I may state, that up to the present moment they have always lived under the same roof. I called on them pretty often; and whatever the hour of my visits—early morning or mid-day or evening—I invariably found all the members of the family not engaged upon some work—men, women, and children—seated round a big *samovar* sipping their weak tea. They always asked me to partake of their refreshment, and they were exceedingly polite and obliging; but, nevertheless, I did not feel at my ease among them. In the mutual relations of the members of the family there was a certain constraint and insincerity. It seemed not only as if I were a stranger amongst them, but that they were all strangers to one another. When I became better acquainted with this family, and with the general conditions of peasant life, I was convinced that my presentiments had not deceived me. There was deep-seated, internal discord in the family, which was only held together partly by the skill of the clever and robust old grandmother, whom all were accustomed to obey, and especially by the unwillingness of each one 'to be the first to begin the row.' It seemed as though each one expected that one of the others should be the first to 'rebel.'

"This discord was of ancient date. It had been worming itself gradually into the heart of the family almost ever since the time when the necessity for earning something extra first became manifest. One of the brothers went to St. Petersburg during the winter months as a cabman, whilst another engaged himself as a forester; but the inequality of their earnings had disturbed the economical harmony of the household. In five months the cabman sent one hundred roubles home to the family, whilst the forester had only earned twenty-five roubles. Now, the question was, Why should he (the forester) consume with such avidity the tea and sugar dearly purchased with the cabman's money? And in general: Why should this tea be absorbed with such greediness by all the numerous members of the household— by the elder brother, for instance, who alone drank something like eighty cups a day (the whole family consumed about nine hundred cups per diem), whilst he did not move a finger towards earning all this tea and sugar? Whilst the cabman was freezing in the cold night air, or busying himself with some drunken passenger, or was being abused and beaten by a policeman on duty near some theatre, this elder brother was comfortably stretched upon his belly, on the warm family oven, pouring out some nonsense about twenty-seven bears whom he had seen rambling through the country with their whelps, in search of new land for settlement. True his (the cabman's) children were fed in the family whilst he was in town; in the summer he was, however, at home, and worked upon their common land with the rest. His children had a right to their bread. The only thing which made him tolerate his dependency was that the horse and the carriage, which he drove when in town, had been purchased out of the common funds. But his endurance did not promise to hold out much longer.

"For two years he had kept silence; but his people were well aware that he tried to 'conceal' a part of his earnings, so that his contribution towards the family income should be pretty much the same as that furnished by the other brothers. When his daughter, a little girl, succeeded in earning fifteen roubles for the family by selling wood-berries, he tried to deduct that amount from his cabman's fees for his own private use. The grandmother would not, however, permit this.

"The next brother (the forester) also began to ponder and to calculate as to how much of his money was 'engrossed' by the eldest brother and his children. A dress for Paranka had been purchased from a pedlar with his money. Now, Paranka was the eldest brother's daughter, and able to earn fifty roubles at work among the osiers, which she appropriated to her own private uses. The forester was very vexed and irritated about the dress bought of the pedlar. As the grandmother took Paranka's side in the dispute, Alexis (the forester) took his next month's salary to the public-house and spent it all in drink.

"It is impossible to describe all these domestic dissensions. The notions as to 'mine' and 'yours,' which disturbed these people's peace of mind, were felt in every trifle—in every lump of sugar, cup of tea, or cotton handkerchief. Nicolas (the cabman) looked at Alexis, thinking, 'You are eating of that which is mine,' conscious, all the while, that at times he, too, had eaten of something belonging to his younger brothers. Alexis, in his turn, could not feel himself quite at his ease. It was all very well for him to hiccough freely after drenching himself with as much tea as he could hold, in sign of his being well pleased and satisfied with himself, after having partaken of tea which was his own, but he was not sincere. A misgiving lurked in his heart, that either in this tea, or in that sugar, or in the white bread, or—which was most certain, and by far the most disagreeable of all—in his own stomach, there was something belonging to somebody else.

"It was exactly this 'mine, thine,' peeping out from every mouthful and from every gulp, which drove me from the Gorshkovs' table, all their obliging invitations to take a cup of tea with them notwithstanding. They drank their tea solemnly and silently, looking steadily into their cups ; but it always seemed to me that they were all trying to drink the same quantity, noting, under the rose, whether any one had out-eaten or out-drunk the others.

"At all events, the sidelong glances they threw upon one another and the children were very bad looks indeed. It was the same in everything. If you hired some horses of one of the brothers for a drive into town, the others, on meeting you, would try to find out how much you had paid him. If you paid one of the brothers his fees the others were sure to stare at your purse and at their brother's hands. Of course such relations could not be maintained for long.

"It so happened that the first to rebel was Paranka. She took it into her head that she could not do without a regular woollen, town-made dress. All the men resisted this whim, for about eighteen months, with resolute energy. A million of times, at least, it was proved to them by the grandmother and the other women, as well as by Paranka herself, who wept bitterly through a number of winter evenings, that no less than a hundred roubles of Paranka's money had been spent upon the family. The men resisted with a truly bull-like stubbornness. Finally, the grandmother herself began to wail, and then the men gave way, and it was resolved that a dress should be made.

"The eldest brother was commissioned to inquire about the prices and everything appertaining to the matter. He resolved to go to the next port, distant about fifteen miles, and to make his inquiries there. He took a provision of oats and hay for the horses, spent two days on the trip, and, having consulted with the smith, the farrier, and several merchants, returned home not one whit the wiser. He did not know how to broach the subject. In order not to allow the brothers to cool down, Paranka had begun to wail incessantly from the very day the resolution as to her dress had been passed at the family council. By dint of these tears she moved the reluctant men to take active steps. The two next brothers put horses into the cart and also went to the port, for there was a saw-mill there, and, in consequence, a large number of people. They were no more fortunate than the elder brother, and came home with the conviction that the women must be sent, for Paranka gave them no peace with her wailings.

The women went and returned perfectly horrified : nobody would think of making a dress such as Paranka wanted for less than forty roubles. Here all the brothers, their wives, and even Paranka herself, seemed to understand that the matter was at an end ; but God saved Paranka. A soldier who happened to be at the port heard about the inquiries of the Gorshkov women, and sent word to the headquarters of a cavalry regiment stationed near Novgorod, some thirty miles off. At these headquarters there was a dressmaker who, profiting by a lucky chance (an officer was transporting a piano to St. Petersburg), begged permission from the carrier to accompany him, and thus arrived at Paranka's village sitting upon the piano. She persuaded the family that all could be well and cheaply arranged.

" But when the brothers counted up everything that had been spent on the dressmaker during the six weeks that she stitched and unstitched the dress, they found that it represented a sum equal in value to the framework of two peasants' houses.

" The dressmaker stole some pieces of stuff, and they had to incur extra expense in recovering them. And worst of all the dress was quite unwearable. Later on, thanks to unremitting toil, and particularly to 'concealment' of money, Paranka succeeding in paying herself for a silk dress by a Novgorod dressmaker, besides a jacket and a paletot. All these treasures she kept hidden in the house of a friend.

"The next after Paranka to squabble was Nicolas, the cabman. He began to urge that he had long since redeemed the carriage and the horse; but the first to break away from the family, and to separate in real earnest, was Alexis, the forester, probably because he felt more sincerely and oftener than the others did the burden of being indebted to others. That part of his own earnings which he considered to be an extra he faithfully spent in drink, that it might fall to nobody's share; he did not, like Nicolas, secrete it. When sober, however, he could not help feeling that he at times ate that which he had not earned. To screw his courage up to break with his family he gave himself up to reckless drinking; he squandered seventy roubles—that is a whole year's salary—at the public-house, and drank himself mad. By this means he was able to tear himself from his own people. In a sober state he would never have had the heart to take his children from the paternal roof-tree, to lead away the cow and the horse, or to pull the slits. He took possession of a small house, built by the Gorshkovs some ten years previously, after a fire, and there he and his family lived whilst a new house was being constructed."

The ultimate complete dissolution of the Gorshkov household is merely a question of time. Thus far there has been no harm in it. The vigour of the big patriarchal families is sapped by the lowest instincts as well as by the loftiest aspirations developed by modern times. They are incompatible with individual independence. Amongst the Southern Russians, with whom the sentiment of individuality is much stronger than among the Great Russians, these composite families are unknown. Their rapid dissolution among the Russians would have been an unmitigated good if it were not accompanied by the general relaxation of social ties between all the members of the village Community.

CHAPTER IV.

For a community of labourers mutual assistance is only another name for mutual insurance. The danger of falling ill or lame, of remaining without support in old age, or of having a "visitation" in the form of fire or murrain, is pretty well equally shared by all. In mutually assisting each other they are doing that which it is to their obvious interest to do; giving the same as they expect in their turn to receive. There is nothing particularly generous in it; nor do they themselves consider it to be anything very meritorious or laudable on their part. Zlatovratsky, in his "Derevenskie Budni" (sketches of every-day village life), describing one of the "old-fashioned" villages, observes how easy it is for an outsider to be led into error if he takes the peasants' statements in a literal sense without observing and investigating for himself.

If, for instance, you were to ask the peasants whether they assist the poor, they would certainly answer, "Oh dear me, no! We are too hard-up ourselves. We throw a *Kopeck*, or a piece of bread, to the poor who knock at our window, that is all." But, if you take the trouble to observe more closely, you are surprised to discover the existence of a vast system of co-operative assistance given to the aged, the orphaned, and the sick, both in field work and in household labour ; only the peasants do not look upon this as charity. It is a simple fulfilment of the obligations of their "daily life." The old man, whose corn the whole *mir* turns out to carry on a Sunday afternoon, receives only what is his due as a *mir's* labourer and tax-payer of several score of years' standing. The orphan receives but a benefit on account of labours to come.

The present increase in the number of purely industrial occupations, which now largely predominate over the agricultural, has made the necessity for this reciprocity less self-evident, and general impoverishment has made its practice hardly possible, even with the best-intentioned. People who live from hand to mouth, and who are compelled to put into requisition every working hour of the day on their own account in order to avert or to postpone their own ruin, cannot afford to be solicitous over any needs but their own. Such considerate mutual assistance, the humanity of which is enhanced by the delicacy with which it is offered, is becoming rarer and rarer. Charity—for our people are still very charitable—is the meagre wraith of the once high conception of co-operative assistance tendered as a duty on the one hand, and accepted as a right on the other.

Enghelhardt gives an exceedingly interesting account of the practice of almsgiving among the peasants of North-Western Russia (White Russian), which under other guises exists in nearly every district of the empire.

" There is no regular distribution by weight of baked bread to beggars, as is, or rather was, the custom in times of yore in the manor-houses. In my house the cook simply gives those who ask 'the morsels,' or small pieces of rye bread, as do all peasants. As long as a *moujik* has one loaf of bread left in his house his wife will give 'morsels.' I gave no orders as to the 'morsels,' and knew nothing about the custom. The cook decided on her own responsibility that 'we' must give 'morsels,' and she accordingly does it.

" In our Province, even after a good season, few peasants are able to make their own bread last until harvest-time comes round again. Almost every family has to buy bread to some extent; and when there is no money for it, the head of the household sends the children, the old men and women 'for morsels.' This year, for instance, the crops were very bad: there was neither bread for the people nor, worse still, forage for the cattle. A man may find food for himself among the people by means of these 'morsels;' but how is he to feed a horse? It cannot be sent from door to door in search of 'morsels.' The outlook is bad, so bad that it cannot well be worse. Most of the children were sent 'for morsels' before St. Cossma and Damian. (1st November: the peasants count the time by the saints' days.) The cold 'St. George' (26th November) in this year proved a hungry one too. There are two 'St. George's' days in the year; the cold—26th November —and the hungry—23rd April, which, falling as it does in the spring, is at a very hungry time of the year. The peasants began to buy bread long before 'St. Nicolas,' which shows that they had not a grain of home-grown corn in the house. For the peasant will never buy any bread until the last pound of flour is kneaded. By the end of December about thirty couples came every day and begged 'for morsels.' Among them were children and old people, also strong lads and maidens. Hunger is a hard master; a fasting man will sell the very saints, say the *moujiks*. A young man or girl feels reluctant and ashamed to beg, but there is no help for it. There is nothing, literally nothing, to eat at home. To-day they have eaten the last loaf of bread, from which they yesterday cut 'morsels' for those who knocked at their door. No bread, no work. Everybody would be happy to work for bare food; but work—why, there is none. A man who seeks 'for morsels' and a regular 'beggar' belong to two entirely different types of people. A beggar is a professional man; begging is his trade. A beggar has no land, no house, no permanent abiding place, for he is constantly wandering from one place to another, collecting bread, eggs, and money: he straightway converts everything he receives in kind—corn, eggs, flour, etc.—into ready money. He is generally a cripple, a sickly man incapable of work, a feeble old man, or a fool:

he is clad in rags, and begs in a loud voice, sometimes in an importunate way, and is not ashamed of his calling. A beggar is God's man. He rarely wanders amongst the *moujiks*, and prefers to haunt towns, fairs, and busy places, where gentlemen and merchants congregate. Professional beggars are rare in the villages ; there they would have little to expect.

"A man, however, who asks 'for morsels' is of quite another class. He is a peasant from the neighbourhood. He is clothed like all his brother peasants, sometimes in a new *armiak;* a linen sack slung over his shoulder is his only distinguishing mark. If he belongs to the immediate neighbourhood even the sack will be missing, for he is ashamed to wear it. He enters the house as if by accident, and on no particular business beyond warming himself a little ; and the mistress of the house, so as not to offend his modesty, will give him 'the morsel' incidentally, and 'unawares.' If the man comes at dinner time he is invited to table. The *moujik* is very delicate in the management of such matters, because he knows that some day he, too, may perhaps have to seek 'morsels' on his own account.

"'No man can forswear either the prison or the

sack,' say the peasants. The man who calls for a 'morsel' is ashamed to beg. On entering the *izba* he makes the sign of the cross and stops on the threshold in silence, or mutters in a low voice, 'Give in Christ's name.' Nobody pays any attention to him; all go on with their business, and chat or laugh as if nobody were there. Only the mistress approaches the table, picks up a piece of bread from three to four square inches in size, and gives it to her visitor. He makes the sign of the cross and goes. All the pieces given are of the same size. If any of the slices given are three square inches in size, all are three square inches. If two people come together (they generally work in couples) the mistress puts the question, 'Are you collecting together?' If the answer is 'Yes,' she gives them a piece of six square inches; if separately, she cuts the piece in two.'"

The man who tramps the neighbourhood thus owns a house, and enjoys his allotted share of land; he is the owner of horses, cows, sheep, clothes, only *for the moment he has no bread.* When in ten months' time he carries his crops, he will not merely cease begging, but will himself be the giver of bread to others; if by means of the aid now afforded him he weathers the storm and succeeds in finding work, he will with the money he earns at once buy bread, and himself help those who have none. This system of asking for help "in kind" serves as a make-shift to avoid the irretrievable ruin which would follow the selling off of his cattle and other property. It is a painful expedient, to which the peasants only resort when all others have failed.

"In the autumn"—we resume the quotation—"when the crops are just gathered, practically all these peasants eat wholemeal rye bread until their hunger is satisfied. Just a few exceptionally prudent families do add husks to their flour even at this season of the year, but such foresight is rare. When, after a time, the head of the family notices that bread is running short, the family has to begin to eat less—perhaps twice a day instead of three times, then only once; the next step is to add husks to the flour. If there is any money left after the taxes are paid, bread is bought; but if there is no money in the house, the head of the household tries to borrow, and pays an enormous interest on any accommodation he gets. Then, when all other means are exhausted, and the last bread has been eaten, the children and the old people swing the sacks over their shoulders and tramp to the neighbouring villages asking help. Whilst the children generally return to sleep at home, their elders go to more remote parts of the country, and return home only after they have collected a considerable number of morsels. On these the family dines, and if there are any left they are first dried in the oven, and then stored away for future use. In the meantime the father is struggling to find work, or to borrow bread, and the mistress is looking after the cattle, and cannot leave the house. The grown-up young people are eager for any employment that will bring in food.

"The father has perhaps succeeded in procuring a few bushels of corn, and in that case the children no longer go to the *mir* and beg from door to door, and the mistress once more distributes 'morsels' to those who knock at theirs. If, on the other hand, the father has failed to procure corn, the children are followed in their piteous quest by the grown-up members of the family, and, finally, by the father himself, who does not go on foot, but with his cart and horse, his wife remaining alone in the house to look after the cattle. The advantage of driving is that the needy men can thus penetrate much further into the country, often even beyond the borders of their Province.

"This winter it has been common enough to meet a cart full of sacks with 'morsels' on the road, and on the cart a *moujik*, a girl, and a boy. Such peasants do not return home before they have collected a considerable supply of bread, which they dry in the oven when stopping to sleep in some village. The family feed on these biscuits, while the father works about the house or seeks for employment somewhere else. When the stock of 'morsels' begins to be exhausted, the horse is once more put into the cart, and they go again on their weary round. Many families provide themselves with food in this way all the winter, and even during a part of the spring; and sometimes, when there is a good supply of these 'morsels' in the house, they are distributed to those who come to beg.

"All this clearly proves that these men are not professional beggars. To them people do not say, when unwilling to give anything themselves, 'God will give you in our stead,' as they do to a regular beggar; but, 'We have nothing to give; we are going to solicit morsels for ourselves.' Another distinction to be drawn between the two classes of beggars is that whereas, as has before been stated, the peasant gives to those in need as soon as he is able, the professional beggar never gives anything to any one.

"Not to give a 'morsel' when there is bread in the house—is a *sin*. That is why my cook gave them without first asking for my permission. Had I forbidden her to do so she would most likely have rebuked me, and in all probability have flatly declined to remain in my service."

In addition to this remarkable development of public-spirited self-sacrifice amongst our peasants, instances occur of yet higher manifestations of the feeling of human brotherhood.

Potanin, in writing of a commune in the Nicolsk district, Province of Vologda, which depended for its support on the work supplied by a salt-house in the neighbourhood, mentions how, in 1878, the firm began to lose ground, and was compelled to reduce the number of the men employed, by one-half. The community, brought face to face with the necessity of seeing one-half of its members condemned to starvation, passed the resolution that each peasant should work only three days in the week instead of six, as heretofore.

It was an heroic impulse which decided these

men to suffer gradually, but together, rather than to snatch the bread from one another's mouths.

As a rule, in all similar cases it has been found that the strongest will outbid the feeblest, and the whole community will look with perfect composure on the ruin of its weaker members.

This power of self-restraint on behalf of the community, has now given place to that cold-blooded indifference to others' woes, to that animal egotism, indicative of a universal breaking up, which has struck with awe many of the observers of modern village life.

There is no secret between fellow villagers concerning their material prosperity. Every peasant knows the exact number of acres tilled by each one of his companions, the number of sacks of grain he has sold, and the number he has kept, and could give an inventory of each household in turn, by heart. If some ill luck befall a family, the village knows exactly what will be the outcome of it. The ruin is foreseen, predicted, expected, with fatal certainty, and takes nobody by surprise.

Here is an excellent peasant family—a husband, wife, two boys, and a girl. It is hard work for the father to feed them all, but he has good helpmates—an industrious, clever wife, and a daughter who has entered upon her sixteenth year. They make both ends meet. The father wishes to find a son-in-law who would consent to live with them, and is looking out for a suitable match for the girl; then the household would be complete. But it chances that the father hurts his leg, and has to keep his bed. This misfortune occurs at the season when work is most pressing, in the spring. The neighbours who have no such affliction to bear, on seeing the piece of ill luck which has befallen the family, cry, "Oh! what a pity, what a pity! Nothing could be worse than to be laid by at the season when work is heaviest. They will now have to sell their two calves to enable them to hire a labourer, and they will be unable to marry their Mariushka."

All this proves true to a fraction. The two calves, destined to defray the expenses of the wedding, are sold, and Mariushka's marriage is postponed. The *batrak* has done his trashy work, and has gone, but the master still remains lying in his bed. An old woman treats him with various home-made medicaments, but the leg grows worse and worse.

In the meantime the mowing season has commenced. Now there is nothing left to sell, to pay for the hiring of a *batrak*. The father makes an effort, rises from his sick bed, sets his scythe, and goes to the field. He mows the hay, but irritates his wounded leg so badly that he falls quite ill, and at about the middle of the harvest time breathes his last.

"Now, say the neighbours, Mariushka must go to town as a servant, to earn money for her mother. There is no use in her remaining at home—nobody will marry her now, poor soul!"

And once more everything happens exactly as had been predicted. Nobody will marry Mariushka, for she cannot leave her family, and no young man will venture to enter into the household as one of its members with so many mouths to feed—two brothers under age, the mother, and his own children into the bargain. So the family remains without a man. But the taxes must be paid for the land, so they resolve to engage a permanent *batrak*. Mariushka goes to town to service to make up enough money for his wages, but she has everything to learn before she can be engaged as a trained servant. Many months pass before she is able to buy herself fitting dresses to wear when she shall have found employment in a "respectable" house. To these difficulties must be added the numberless uncertainties and temptations besetting a young girl in a town. She may be seduced, and return with a baby to the village, and a life of eternal shame. A mere accident: the gentleman in whose family she was engaged as servant has lost his employment, and for three months is unable to pay her her wages, so that Mariushka cannot send a penny home to her mother just at the time when money is the most urgently needed. Arrears in the taxes accumulate upon the arrears of the wages due to the *batrak*.

The land is taken from the mother, and her cow is sold to pay the *batrak*. What could the poor woman do in this extremity? She has two boys to bring up, one of ten the other of eleven years of age. They are not workers as yet, but they need to be fed, and the mother has nothing to give them. Her only expedient is to send them also to town to Mariushka, who is glad to find them employment with a publican.

The mother remains alone. She is sick at heart, weary of this life of suffering and wretchedness. She sells the house and goes away, a sack on her shoulders, to the shrine of some saint, there to pray for the soul of her deceased husband, and for the two boys who are pining away in the tavern, and for Mariushka too, of whom nothing whatever has been heard. " Oh, poor creature ! " say the neighbours pityingly, as they see the owner of the ruined nest off; and a week later they welcome the new proprietors of the house. The recent drama is forgotten.

Or another case—two brothers. The elder, Nicolas, is a hard-working, indefatigable *moujik*, but he can hardly keep body and soul together, and is gnawing his heart out in vain efforts to improve his condition. Opposite him lives his brother Aleshka, a bumpkin, who never yet succeeded in anything. This Aleshka was employed as a forest surveyor, at seven roubles per month. Nicolas has ousted him. Aleshka occasionally takes a drop too much, whilst Nicolas is a total abstainer. " It is just the same to Aleshka whether he earns money or not," he said.

Ousted from this employment, Aleshka tries the wood trade, and delivers fire-wood at certain places. Nicolas " finds out " the wood-yard, offers his services at a lower price, and ousts his brother again. "What right has he to grumble?"

he asked; "I do not hinder him from offering his services at a yet cheaper rate."

And what of their fellow-villagers, the *mir?* What are they doing? They look on with perfect equanimity, merely stating the facts—"John must go begging." "Peter will flourish." "Andrew will have to starve," and so on.

When Nicolas turned his brother out of his situation in the forest, " Seven roubles a month will be a God-send to Nicolas!" remarked the neighbours. " Now he will thrive apace." When Aleshka was ousted by his brother from the wood trade, and shortly afterwards lost to him a small meadow, rented from a landlord, the neighbours said, "Now Aleshka is lost, he must come to downright ruin." And Aleshka could not help ratifying their prognostication. He has a lot of children, one under another, and a sickly wife, unfortunately endowed with great fecundity. Aleshka, on seeing ruin and desolation creeping over him, gave himself up to drinking, and began to beat his wife furiously, in the hope that it might subdue her untoward fecundity, and bring it to a level with his miserable means. In this he did not succeed, and then threw the heft after the hatchet by drinking more than ever. On seeing him stretched in the mud in the gutter, face downwards, motionless as a log, people predicted, "He will be found thus some day, dead." Aleshka, however, escaped death, and a new and terrible misfortune overtook him.

One day the news spread through the village that Aleshka's three daughters, left by the mother to the care of their elder brother, a boy of nine (the father was absent also, stealing wood from the landlord's forest), had, in playing, upset a boiling samovar, and had scalded themselves from head to foot, "In a few hours they will probably be dead," prophesied the village experts. As, however, in villages everything is known and so very many things foreseen, this prophecy was accompanied by another. "Why! perhaps now Aleshka may improve his position. Certainly it is hard upon him to have to bear such a blow, for who does not pity his own flesh and blood? But, on the other hand, nobody can pry into God's designs. Who knows but what God in his wisdom—— At all events Aleshka will have a chance; certainly his prospects may improve."

As a matter of fact the children did die, and, as a matter of fact also, Aleshka did begin to improve.

Such are the incidents which sometimes "save" a peasant from inevitable ruin! Each for himself. Near is my shirt, but nearer is my skin. The commune has been transformed into a pack of galley slaves, each of whom endeavours to minimise his share of the burden and responsibilities.

The commune asks for an advance from the *zemstvo*. The *zemstvo* accedes to the demand, and sends in a subsidy only sufficient, as a matter of course, to assist the needy families. In a village composed of some twenty households there are, let us say, five families which are destitute. The money, or the provision of corn, sent by the *zemstvo* is accordingly sufficient to relieve only these five families. But the subsidy is advanced to the *mir* as a whole, under its collective responsibility. The *zemstvo* cannot have dealings with, or rely upon the solvency of, Peter or of John, and other private individuals who may be soliciting its assistance. Now, as the whole village is answerable for the cost of the supplies sent, the peasants say, "If I shall have to pay, let me have my share too." It is resolved, therefore, at the *mir's* meeting that the subsidy shall be divided amongst all, apportioning, moreover, the shares according to the number of "souls" in each household. The "soul" which is the unit for measuring the working capacities of each household (as well as the amount of land apportioned to it), at the same time represents the liability of each household with regard to all those taxes and payments and duties of any kind, which fall on the commune in a lump.

Thus, in the distribution of the *zemstvo's* subsidy, the richest family, which represents five "souls," and has five shares of land, will receive most of the corn; the medium-sized, representing three souls, will have three shares. As to the landless *bobyl*, who is economically a cipher, because he does not stand even for a fraction of a "soul," he receives nothing at all, though he may have the largest family and be the most needy. People do not want to be answerable for him. If he is reluctant to resort to the usual expedient of "going for morsels," he must re-borrow the subsidy at its full valuation, and upon his own responsibility, from his well-to-do neighbours, who have received it without any individual payment.

No wonder that the barefooted horde in its turn shows no particular goodwill to its well-to-do fellow-villagers.

Ivan Ermolaeff grumbles. He is a typical "*grey moujik*," this Ivan Ermolaeff. Though with a slight leaning towards the *koulaks*, he retains all the traditions and tastes of a genuine peasant in their full intensity, and hates and despises all non-agricultural profits as unbecoming a *moujik*. He is far cleverer than another "*grey moujik*" of our acquaintance, Ivan Afanasieff, whom we introduced to the reader in a former chapter.

Whilst puny Ivan Afanasieff, with all his diligence and ardent love for the land, is unmistakably on the high road to become a landless *batrak*, energetic and ready-witted Ivan Ermolaeff will certainly hold his own, at all events for many years to come.

Working all the year round like a galley slave, Ivan Ermolaeff makes both ends meet, and "does not suffer from hunger," which is the *beau ideal* of a *grey moujik*.

Yet he grumbles. He grumbles, not against his hard lot, which he supports with stoical endurance, but against the people, against his fellow-villagers.

"You try to improve your position, and your neighbours do their best to ruin you."

"How can that be? Why should they do it?"

"I do not know; since they do do it, they must certainly have some reason. 'You are doing well, I am doing badly.' 'Well, let us so arrange matters that you shall do badly too.' 'It will put all upon the same level.' 'Judge for yourself. We have here a forest belonging to the Commune. Everybody receives a part of it for his own personal use. Well, I have hewn my wood, grubbed up the ground, have generally improved it, and transformed it into arable land. As soon as I have by my own labour obtained more land, they shout, 'Let us have a redistribution! You hold more land than those who pay for the same number of souls. The quantity of communal land has increased; let us have a redistribution!'"

"But is not everybody free to reclaim his part of the waste land?"

"Yes, but everybody is not willing to do it. Herein lies the difference—some are not strong enough, others are too lazy. I am up before the dawn, I work in the sweat of my brow, I harvest more crops. Oh! they will take it from me, you may depend upon it. "And do you think it will be of any great advantage to them?" "Not at all. Each will receive a bagatelle, a mere strip, a narrow slip of land. They have twice played me this same trick. It is useless to try to improve my position."

"And are there many people in your village who are thus hindering you?"

"Certainly, many. The rich bar my way, and the poor bar my way likewise."

A new stream of feeling, which is anything but benevolent, is springing up in the villages amongst the disinherited "victims" of the social struggle, which bodes evil both to social order and to their victorious brethren.

Formerly the peasants used to hate their masters, the nobles, and the *tchinovniks*, who, rod in hand, managed the manorial estates. This hatred, however bitter, fell on outsiders, who formed a small body of people, who were allowed to oppress and torture the peasants by the Tzar's sufferance, not by any power of their own.

At the present day the bitterest enemies to the people are singled out from among their own ranks. They form a detached and numerous class, which has its adherents, and agents, and supporters. The hatred they inspire in millions of the peasants is as legitimate as that inspired by the slave-owning nobility in times of yore. Modern hatred assumes the character of class-hatred, and extends to the whole social system, of which the rural plutocracy is the necessary outcome.

CHAPTER V.

"Every time I happen to meet or to speak to the peasant Havrila Volkov," says Uspensky, " I invariably think how dreadful it will be to witness the time when this Volkov shall let loose the fierce hatred and rage which lie hidden in the depths of his heart, and are at present only discovered in the cruel expression of his eyes and mouth, and by the harsh tones of his voice. For when the outward pressure which holds him down shall be removed, his hidden passions will immediately assume the form of a powerful, revengeful, and pitiless giant, raising an enormous cudgel against everything and everybody.

"A man of herculean strength, Havrila Volkov is also undoubtedly endowed with great mental energy. But the transition period through which we are passing, though already protracted to such an abnormally long time, has provided no solid food for the popular intelligence to digest ; indeed, hardly any food at all, because during all this time nothing has been so thwarted and obstructed as the influences which might have resulted in a sound development of the popular intelligence. Owing to this, Havrila's mind is only distorted, disconcerted, unhealthily excited by vague rumours and hopes, and as unhealthily depressed by other rumours of an opposite nature. 'Money'—this is the only immutably solid thing amidst all the contradictions and uncertainties of life.

" Havrila is now about forty years of age. He was born, and grew into young manhood, in the days of serfdom, though people were already talking about the coming Emanicipation.

"These rumours grew more persistent, and with them the hopes for the future grew stronger and brighter. Serfdom was at last abolished. Their lord, whom Havrila's parent served, mortgaged his estate and disappeared. The manor house stood deserted and locked up. The hateful past seemed to be blotted out for ever. Yet people had to work harder than before, because the peasants' land had been curtailed and their expenses had increased. They could not live by the land alone, and were forced to go to town to seek work there. Havrila's family, however, ruled by a hard and despotic father, preserved a comparative affluence, because kept together by the strong hand of its head; but it was trying to have to bear his despotism. He took all the money earned by his sons. One brother earned more, another less, for equal skill was not required for their respective work.

"They were all put on an equal footing by the absolute rule of their father, which appeared to Havrila to be nothing less than wanton tyranny. To become rich through husbandry had gone out of fashion. The method which had come to be much in vogue was to gain wealth by speculation and by usury. A constant rage was gnawing at Havrila's heart: the family had eaten up such a lot of his own earnings, that, if he had used it in speculative ventures, he might by that time have been as rich and as respected as their neighbour Cheremukhin, who had started in business with a solitary sixpence in his pocket. Domestic despotism oppressed him to no purpose. By agricultural work, however hard, it was futile to try to match Cheremukhin's profits.

As time moved on, the despotic habits of the father, instead of taming down, became daily more oppressive. Taxes were increasing, the family stood in need of more money—*ergo*, the work grew heavier and heavier, otherwise the greater expenditure could not be met, and Cheremukhin would swallow them up. All this only stirred up Havrila's rage the more. His father ought to let him live by himself on his own earnings, and after what fashion he liked. But the old man would not hear of it, and squeezed him ever closer in the effort to make both ends meet.

"Yet all this relentless work notwithstanding, ruin was always imminent. If by ill luck the horse should one day perish, they would be compelled to implore Cheremukhin's assistance, and it would be all over with their independence. But just look at Cheremukhin; he could impose his yoke on everybody, whilst nobody could impose a yoke on him, and he was a stranger to poverty and hard labour.

"To what purpose all this? Wherefore this eternal drudgery, which gave neither ease nor independence in return? Havrila and his brothers had on several occasions tried to rebel against their father's despotism, but had learned that this despotism was strong, and had moreover the support of the *mir*, who could flog the irreverent sons. Rancour brooded in Havrila's heart,—rancour against his father, against work, and against taxation, resentment towards Cheremukhin, and envy of his easily-won wealth; indignation at the paucity of land, and the multitude of rates and taxes imposed upon the peasants. For ever working, for ever paying, without any profit for yourself or for the household. There was only one thing that Havrila understood with perfect clearness, *i.e.*, that *money* was the solution of all problems, and the means wherewith all difficulties might be settled. One needed only to make money. With money you were free as a bird; you could buy everything, sell it, and buy it back again.

"At last the despotic father died. Havrila immediately separated from the others, and he and his wife started a new household. He had no faith left in agriculture, which had become hateful to him; yet he was still compelled to live by this work, and under far more distressing conditions than before. Thenceforth he was the only full-grown labourer in the household. Instead of rising to it, as he had expected, he sank immeasurably below the level of his ideal, Cheremukhin. After his separation he could hardly keep the wolf from the door. All the year round he dwelt in dirt, in poverty, and in interminable, ungrateful work, without hope or respite.

"A passionate desire to make their way in the world absorbed all the thoughts of Havrila and his wife,—an energetic and stern woman. They must have money, no matter by what means. No kind of swindling came amiss to Havrila provided it promised to forward his aim—wealth. He had heard that Cheremukhin pressed hay and sold it at a profit in St. Petersburg. He was also told that damaged hay often passed undetected amongst the good—who can see what is put into the middle of a bundle of hay? Havrila commenced to speculate in rotten hay. He found customers, and at first sold them several cart-loads of sound hay, then palmed off a lot of spoilt stuff all in one consignment, and then disappeared. He repeated this operation successfully with several people in different parts of St. Petersburg, and had begun to make a little money, though the amount was very small as yet, when one day he was caught in the act, dragged to the Police Station, and indicted before a Magistrate. He lied and prevaricated like any conjurer, but could not exculpate himself, and was locked up, and lost both hay and money.

"Swindling had proved a failure, though he knew by many examples that this was not always so. Exasperated by his losses and his humiliation, Havrila applied his mind with redoubled energy to the discovery of some new means whereby he might retrieve his fortunes. He eagerly caught at any information which bore in any way upon money-making. Events at St. Petersburg (*i.e.*, the attempt against the Emperor's life) gave rise to a great many vague and irritating rumours amongst the masses. One day, on passing by a manorial wood, Havrila met a gentleman in a gig, a gun slung behind his shoulders, and a wild duck, just shot, lying at the foot of the box. With one flash all the wickedness and spite which lay fermenting in Havrila's head and soul broke forth into a brutal desire 'to catch the gentleman and hand him over to justice. It is all the work of gentlemen (*i.e.* these attempts) who are set against the Tzar. I will earn a reward. . . . Poaching in the Tzar's woods . . . first-rate chance . . . a reward!' And Havrila, though perfectly indifferent to the interests of the Crown, forthwith flew at the gentleman, like a robber, snatched at his gun and the duck, climbed into the gig, and, seizing the reins, drove him as a prisoner at full speed to the village. . . 'A gentleman without a passport . . . caught by me in the Tzar's woods . . .

identify him!' shouted Havrila, with the evident desire of making as much noise and scandal as possible.

"When the superintendent officer had listened to Havrila's exultant report of his exploit he warned him : ' I shall advise this gentleman to take an action out against you for violent assault. Out of my sight, you idiot!' Havrila did as a matter of fact have to appear before the magistrate, but the gentleman spared him, and he therefore bowed low to him, craving his pardon, whilst in his breast he was boiling over with rage against the gentleman, the authorities, and his own stupidity.

"' No,' he secretly resolved, 'one must rob. There is nothing for it but to rob.'

"An intense desire to appropriate things belonging to others, particularly money, assumed in him the strength of a devouring passion. Side by side with this covetousness there grew upon Havrila and his wife, who understood her husband's wishes at a glance, a kind of austere avarice. They had never spent a penny on tea or sugar ; since Havrila had separated from his relatives he had not smoked one ounce of tobacco nor drunk one glass of brandy. Never did he exchange a friendly word with anybody, unless expecting to reap some profit by it. If he had called on you he would have squeezed something out of you in some way or other before he left, on that you might depend. He would literally compel you to submit to the necessity of being cheated by him. His object once attained, he would not stop at your house one minute longer; but in case of failure he would drink three samovars, and sit for five hours as dumb as an idol, until he had contrived to gain at least some of his ends.

"If he had nothing to expect from you he would pay you no attention, perhaps not recognise you at all. On looking at his cruel face and harsh eyes, which made every attempt to smile 'like a peasant' simply pitiful, one felt that a reserve of strength that boded no good, lay hidden in this dark soul.

"A dark night, a deserted, out-of-the-way thoroughfare, a drunken wayfarer with a bundle of banknotes in his pocket, and a blow with an iron pole-axe on the temple, must have often flashed through this energetic but benighted brain as the 'real thing,' the only solution to all difficulties.

"Cherishing such ideas and such feelings as

these in his breast, Havrila was nevertheless compelled to drudge away at the land. He had three children, all under age, and he worked briskly and vigorously, though sullenly. He kept down the bile and spite and rage which were devouring him, but he gnawed at the bit. When his opportunity came he would give rein to his rebellious temper, and would take a frightful revenge for the enforced submissiveness of years, and for the trampling down of his own natural feelings, for the slow murder of his two 'superfluous' children, dispatched by himself and his wife to the other world as untoward obstacles; for the humiliations of poverty, and for the galling drudgery of hateful toil."

Another interesting character in Uspensky's gallery, Ivan Bosykh, is a person of totally different temper and nature. He is, indeed, the kindest and the most benevolent of men. But he is one of the regular "victims" in the economical struggle, and the trying circumstances of his position have exasperated him to such an extent as to have converted him into certainly quite as dangerous a character as Havrila.

"Ivan Bosykh belongs," says Uspensky, "to that useless and miserable class of beings whose existence is incomprehensible, even disgraceful in a country like Russia, but who nevertheless do exist, and during the last twenty years have been constantly on the increase, a class which, willingly or unwillingly, must be designated as 'rural proletariats.'

" Bosykh, when sober, is the kindest of men and an excellent worker, having 'golden hands,' as the peasants say nowadays. However, he is rarely seen to advantage. Only a few years ago it was otherwise. Then Ivan Bosykh was in all respects an exemplary *moujik*, and his household, though not rich, was united and orderly —' pleasant to behold,' to use his fellow-villagers' expression. Now he is the poorest *batrak* in the village. His cottage is fallen into decay. The window-panes are broken, and the gaps stopped up with dirty rags. He beats his wife, a clever, industrious woman, and remarkably beautiful, whom he married for love. She took a summons out against him. His three ragged children wander about the village all day long, cared for by nobody, and hungry. If you make enquiries about him in the village you will receive the most unfavourable references. He has sold the same hay three times over to three different persons, and spent all the money in drink. He borrowed money on his heifer in three different shops, but paid it over to none of them, having sold it meanwhile to a fourth and spent the money, as usual, in drink.

The history of Ivan Bosykh's ruin and moral degradation is instructive because it is so commonplace—hundreds of thousands of Ivan Bosykhs have been ruined in exactly the same manner. If Bosykh fell lower than some, it was merely because, being more sensitive, he was more subject to despair.

The chief instruments of his ruin were as usual the village usurers, the *koulaks*. It began slowly at first. To begin with, his land was curtailed, the meadow and pasture lands were retained by the landlord, whilst the taxes in the meantime were increased, a common, oft-repeated story. With a young family like his, Ivan Bosykh could not avoid the necessity of now and then applying for small loans to fill up the gaps in his balance sheet.

"' Then,' he explains, 'one creditor bothers you for one rouble, another for two. You make shift and pay—with interest. Interest here, interest there—and lo! there is a new gap which you had not noticed before.'

For a long time Ivan Bosykh struggled bravely against heavy odds, which he thought would be only temporary, and kept himself more or less above water, when a 'sudden visitation' overtook him and felled him to the ground. His two horses and his cow were killed by the murrain. In this desperate position Ivan Bosykh applied to a regular *koulak*, his brother-in-law. By dint of supplication and the intercession of his sister Ivan Bosykh bought a horse from his brother-in-law, on credit, for thirty-five roubles, to be paid in the spring, though the beast had cost the *koulak* no more than fifteen roubles. But Ivan accepted this deliverance even at that price, and thanked his kinsman most humbly for his kindness.

As he had only one horse to feed, his brother-in-law offered to buy his hay. Ivan Bosykh, greatly pressed for money as he was, agreed to part with his hay for five kopecks per stone. Soon after he had to dispose of his heifer, as he could not feed it well after the death of his cow. His brother-in-law bought it for five roubles, and a few weeks later Bosykh learned that he had resold it for twenty-five roubles. He also learned that the hay he had parted with at five kopecks per stone had been resold in the town for twenty kopecks, his brother-in-law making a net profit of full eleven kopecks per stone.

When Bosykh, after having delivered a lot of hay to his brother-in-law, tried to get rid of him, as he had a perfect right to do, and found another hay merchant, willing to pay him a more reasonable price—ten kopecks per stone—his brother-in-law grew furious, and charged him with base ingratitude. Another *koulak*, Parfenoff by name, the man who had packed Bosykh's hay, and whom in hanging his customer Bosykh had 'robbed' of a part of his profits, made common cause with his brother-in-law. Together they tried to enforce obedience on their common victim.

As Bosykh refused to sell for five kopecks what he could sell for ten, they resolved to take the horse from him; without a horse he would be altogether prevented from working his farm. The brother-in-law and Parfenoff tried to lead off the horse from Bosykh's house by force. A scuffle ensued, in which Bosykh proved to be the strongest. Upon this the brother-in-law lodged a complaint against Bosykh before the village tribunal. Here Parfenoff was one of the judges, and the other judges were his friends. A glass of wine here, a bottle of beer there—the verdict was : to take the horse from the defendant, and to give him twenty strokes with the rod for having boxed Parfenoff and his own brother-in-law on the ears.

"'I was not present at the trial,' said Ivan Bosykh. 'After the verdict a policeman was sent to my house : "You must go to the *volost*," he said. "What for?" "You are to be flogged." "Oh, no, not I." "Yes, you are, though." "No, I won't. Tell them to flog somebody else, if they like." I grew quite furious,' he continued. How is this?' said I to myself; 'our lords flogged us when we were serfs, and now, when that is over, a simple *moujik* like myself can flog me because I will not voluntarily allow him to rob me of my own! I gave this scoundrel (brother-in-law) one hundred roubles' worth of my toil, but he requires more, and means to flog me into obedience."

Bosykh resolved to make a firm stand for his rights. The horse was his rightful property by the terms of his agreement, whereby payment for it became due in the following spring, six months hence. He appealed against the judgment of the village Court, and declared that he would not give up the beast. But it was easier to come to this resolution than to keep it. A few days later the brother-in-law, Parfenoff, and the village elder, who was also a *koulak* of the same stamp, entered his house, breaking the door of the house open with an improvised battering-ram, as well as those of the stable, where the horse lay hidden, and led it away in triumph.

"'You expected that we should await the decision of the Court?' said the elder, who led the band. 'No! with such knaves as you we conduct things in a more speedy fashion—mind that! And you will be flogged into the bargain, take my word for it. Perhaps you want to lodge a complaint against me? Please try it. We have sentenced you to twenty lashes now; after that you will receive a hundred and twenty.' On this they retired.

" Thus,' says Bosykh, 'I was left without my horse, and such a rage took possession of me that it seemed as though the very devil had entered into my body. My wife began to weep over our ruin; I flew at her like a madman. By God! I do not know how I could have had the heart to raise my hand against her. She began to cry, and this only increased my fury. I left her at last and ran straight to the tavern.

Here I promised the inn-keeper to sell him my hay, at two kopecks a stone, provided he would give me wine, and I drank and drank till I lost my senses. I could not reach my house, but stumbled into a ditch, with my face in the mud, and fell asleep. How long I lay there I do not know. The cold awakened me, and I opened my eyes. The moon was up; in the village the girls were singing their songs. I arose. In passing by Parfenoft's house I saw the whole party through the window,—the elder and my brother-in-law among them, grouped round the table, on which stood a boiling samovar and a bottle of wine. They were celebrating their triumph. All my fury returned at once. I rushed into Parfenoft's house just as I was, besmeared with mud, and barefoot, because I had left my boots at the tavern in exchange for drink. I went straight up to the elder, and treated him to a sound rap on the snout; then I did the same to Parfenoff, and then to my brother-in-law. They rushed at me. But no! I was quite in earnest this time. "I will kill you, you damned scoundrels!" I shouted. "Give me wine, you rascals!" All my strength returned to me at this moment. I should have crushed, with one blow, the first who had dared to approach me, and they knew it, too, for they left me alone and sent for help. I sat at the table, drank up the wine, and then with the empty bottle struck the looking-glass, which fell to pieces, and in its descent knocked the tea-tray on to the floor.

"'In the meantime help had arrived. They knocked me down, bound my hands, and put me under lock and key. All three sent in their complaints against me. I was summoned to appear before the tribunal, but I would not go, and went to the tavern instead. They passed a verdict of "contumacy" against me, and sentenced me to be flogged. They summoned me for the execution of the sentence. I would not go. They sent for me three times. I spat in their messenger's face and told him that I would not go. In defence of their three snouts they sentenced me to upwards of one hundred strokes. I held fast to my resolution not to submit. Thank God there were other good people in the village to support me. Thus I succeeded in escaping from their clutches up to Lady Day, my chief consolation in the meanwhile being the tavern. By this time my new friend, the merchant to whom I had agreed to deliver the hay, began to threaten me with a writ. But how could I bring my hay into the town when I had no horse? Besides which the tavern-keeper required the same hay, because I owed it to him for drink. I could not look people in the face for very shame.

"When Lady Day had passed I heard the tinkling of little bells, and saw three *troikas* (carriages driven by three horses) running into the village. It was the elder, the judges, and the *stanovoi*. My heart sank within me at the sight. They stopped just before my gate, entered my house, and called a village meeting. "The taxes!" No means to escape was left me. People began to bring their taxes, and the elder approached the *stanovoi*, and pointing to me said, "This peasant, your Excellency, was four times sentenced by the tribunal for having insulted, first his brother-in-law, then me, then Parfenoff, and then his brother-in-law again. He was twenty times summoned to attend at the *volost*, but he will not obey and offers resistance. Moreover he does not pay his taxes. Will you permit us to execute the verdict at once?"

"'It was then that they laid me down. It was then that I lost my reason, and my shame, and my conscience. I lay on the ground like a log, and they lashed me, and lashed me again, in virtue of all four resolutions. I lay there, and, will you believe it? I was frightened of myself! By God, yes! frightened of myself, frightened to jump to my feet, frightened to move, lest I should slay the first whom my hand could reach.

"'At last I perceived that the hounds had taken rather a liking to the operation.

"'Enough!' I cried, and in such a voice that they stopped at once, the damned scoundrels!

"'Well, from that time forth I was a lost man. Lost—absolutely lost! Everything became disgusting to me, the work, the house, the light of day. The tavern grew to be my only consolation. I began even to steal! Everything went from bad to worse, and I doubt now whether there will ever again be any chance for me to retrieve myself. Something dreadful will happen, I am sure. I am quite beside myself from exasperation. A mortal anguish is gnawing at my heart. The evil one is whispering in my ear. Oh! he will incite me to something horrible. I shall end in the galleys, take my word for it.'"

Ivan Bosykh is one sample drawn from a number,—an illustration of the feelings which are surging in the hearts of our toiling millions. This state of things must naturally lead to some practical manifestation on the part of the disinherited.

The "red cock," or wilful arson of another man's property, this favourite means of revenge within the power of the weak of heart, is no rare guest in modern Russian villages. Our meek and patient peasantry are, however, beginning to learn even fiercer methods of retaliation. There is ample evidence in the reports of foreign correspondents (Russian papers are not allowed to mention such delicate subjects) that agrarian crimes like those at one time of such frequent occurrence in Ireland are beginning to strike root upon Russian soil. Sometimes they assume the character of a solemn public execution. The most striking so far, has been that recently perpetrated by the peasants of a village in the Insar district (Province of Pensa), who at their public meeting passed a resolution to put the land-agent of their landlord to death, and went in a body and carried this resolution into effect. For this offence fourteen peasants were sentenced to death in October 1887 by a Court Martial, and two were actually hanged on November 24th,—a drastic sentence, and a drastic proceeding, evidently intended to strike terror into the peasantry, because according to Russian law and every day practice, all crimes, save political ones, are tried before a jury, and there is no capital punishment for any common offence.

Still, if we take into consideration the enormity of the popular sufferings, and the paucity of agrarian crime and agrarian disturbance of any kind, we must admit that the Russian peasants practically keep very quiet.

Where lies the source of this phenomenal endurance displayed by a mass of several scores of millions of people, whose bitter dissatisfaction with their lot admits of no shadow of doubt?

In the character of our race? In our people's past history or present political superstitions? Each of these causes must certainly have had its share of influence, though they are but secondary ones, which cannot explain this strange fact satisfactorily. We, for our part, think that the main cause of it lies elsewhere, and is this : the moral, political, and social discontent seething in the heart of the rural population of Russia has found a sort of safety-valve in the new evolution of religious thought which nowadays covers almost the whole field of the intellectual activity of the Russian labouring classes. Almost the whole moral and intellectual force produced by the modern Russian peasantry runs in the channel of religion; religion engrosses the leading minority of the people who understand most thoroughly and feel most keenly the evils of the day, and who alone would be able to put themselves at the head of any vast popular movement. That religion should play this part of intercessor between popular discontent and its logical outcome—open rebellion—is all the more natural and unavoidable inasmuch as our new popular religions are not merely a protest against, but to some extent a cure to, the evils against which the popular conscience is the most indignant. The religious enthusiasm proper to all new sects has re-established —for a time at least— more fraternal relations between those men who adhere to them, and has subdued the fierce and cynical struggle for economical predominance which is raging in our villages.

This interesting process we will endeavour to investigate in its fulness in the following studies upon popular religion.

www.ingramcontent.com/pod-product-compliance
Lightning Source LLC
Chambersburg PA
CBHW031433230426
43668CB00007B/516